Contract Bridge:

HOW TO IMPROVE
YOUR TECHNIQUE

Contract Bridge:

How to Improve Your Technique

BY ROBERT B. EWEN

FRANKLIN WATTS, INC. • NEW YORK, 1975

7101802

Library of Congress Cataloging in Publication Data

Ewen, Robert B.   1940-

    Contract bridge.

    (A Concise guide)
    Bibliography: p.
    1. Contract bridge. I. Title.
GV1282.3.E88   795.4'152   74-9620
ISBN 0-531-02787-2

Contents

Preface

This book is for people who have played some bridge and know the rudiments of the game, and who want to improve their technique without wading through huge volumes or studying for hundreds of hours. Some memory work *is* necessary in order to play bridge well, but too much of it can spoil anyone's fun. Therefore I have tried wherever possible to explain the logic behind what you are advised to do, so that you can enjoy the challenge of bridge by learning to think like an experienced player.

Although basic in scope, this book contains enough important ideas so that you'll be well within the top half of all bridge players if you know how to use them all. *Don't* try to rush through the book in an evening or two; take your time, think over what you read, and discuss it with your favorite partner(s).

Good luck!

Bob Ewen

The Opening Bid

It's more fun to open the bidding than to pass, but a certain amount of discretion is advisable. If you open with insufficient values, you're likely to wind up writing down unpleasantly large numbers on the opponents' side of the score sheet. Even worse, you'll have to face one of the most dangerous beasts known to mankind — an angry partner.

In this chapter, therefore, we'll look at methods for correctly evaluating the strength of your hand, including some expert tips that will polish up your bridge technique. Once we have discussed *when* to open the bidding, we'll move on to *what* you should bid when you do open.

HAND EVALUATION

All 13-point bridge hands are equal, a famous author once wrote, but some are more equal than others. Which of the following hands would you rather hold?

(1)	♠ 8 7 6 4 3	(2)	♠ K Q 8 7 6
	♡ J 9 7 4 3		♡ A J 9 7 3
	◇ K Q		◇ 6 3
	♣ A		♣ 4

Let's *count our points* in each case:

High-Card Points (HCP)	Distribution Points (DP)
Ace = 4	Void = 3
King = 3	Singleton = 2
Queen = 2	Doubleton = 1
Jack = 1	

Apparently, each hand is worth 10 high-card points (HCP) — 4 for the ace, 3 for the king, 2 for the queen, and 1 for the jack — and 3 distribution points (DP) — 2 for the singleton club and 1 for the doubleton diamond — or a total of 13 points. Obviously, then, the two hands are equally strong and should be bid exactly the same way, right?

Wrong!

To see why, suppose your partner has the following hand:

♠ A 5 2
♡ Q 10 8
◇ A 7 4
♣ Q 8 6 2

If you have hand (1), you don't have a ghost of a chance of making game; you're sure to lose at least two spade tricks and two heart tricks. With hand (2), however, game in spades or hearts is an excellent contract and should definitely be bid.

Since partner has the same hand in both cases, we can't blame this confusion on him. Clearly, hand (2) must be considerably stronger than hand (1). And, therefore, you must bid these hands differently in order to reach the right contract. Hand (2) is actually worth around 14 or 15 points; and since all hands worth 14 or more points should be opened, you should bid 1 ♠ with this hand. Hand (1), however, is actually worth only about 11 or 12 points; and since hands worth 12 points or less should not be opened, you should pass if you hold this hand.

The reason for this apparent contradiction is that while point count is a fairly accurate guide to the potential trick-taking strength of a bridge hand, it is far from perfect. HCP and DP are good not in and of themselves, but because having more of these points usually does mean that you will be able to take more tricks when the deal is eventually played out. (Remember that in bridge the score comes from taking enough tricks — and *not* from having a lot of HCP and DP!) But there are times when the point-count method springs a leak, and overvalues or undervalues the trick-taking ability of your hand.

Attempts have been made to build appropriate corrections into the point count itself, but the results turned out to be so complicated that only an Einstein could remember them. Unless you happen to enjoy memorizing huge lists of "adjustments," or struggling with fractional point counts such as $14\frac{1}{2}$ or $16\frac{5}{8}$, the best way to improve your ability to evaluate the strength of a bridge hand is to become familiar with the exceptional cases. Then, when you spot an unusually good holding, you can simply add an extra point or two; and when you recognize an unusually poor holding, all you need do is subtract a point or two. This may not be accurate enough to satisfy a mathematician, but it will get you to the right contract more often without spoiling your fun.

Here, then, are the special cases to watch for:

1. *It's good to have all your high cards in your long suits, and it's bad to have all your high cards in your short suits.* In the example at the beginning of this chapter, hand (2) should be upgraded because all the high cards are in the long suits, where their trick-taking power will help out the many small cards in those suits. Hand (1), however, should be downgraded because just about all of the high cards are in the short suits, where they won't do as much good.

2. *It's bad to have honors that aren't sufficiently protected.* Consider the following holdings:

Singleton K, Q, or J
Doubleton KQ, KJ, or QJ

If the opponents should have the ace and lead it, you'll have to sacrifice an honor because you don't have any small cards in the suit. Since your honors may not pull their full weight during the play, it's a good idea to deduct about 1 point for each such holding that you have. Hand (1) at the beginning of this chapter therefore warrants an extra deduction.

3. *Short suits are worthless if you plan to play in no-trump.* Short suits don't win tricks. They are worth points only because the sooner you run out of a suit, the sooner you can insert a trump and stop the opponents from running an unpleasantly large number of tricks. In a no-trump contract, however, you can't ruff anything, so *don't* count any distribution points for your short suits if it becomes apparent that you're going to wind up in no-trump. For example, suppose your partner opens the bidding with 1 NT and you hold:

♠ K 10
♡ 7 4
♢ A 10 8 7
♣ J 9 5 3 2

Game in a minor suit requires 11 tricks and game in no-trump requires only 9 tricks, and your hand is reasonably balanced. You should therefore plan to remain in no-trump, and evaluate your hand as worth 8 points (8 HCP, 0 DP).

4. *Short suits are especially good when you have excellent support for partner's suit (and plan to play there).* If you plan to play in your partner's suit and have plenty of trumps, your short suits are likely to be especially useful because you'll be able to ruff several times. In such cases, therefore, count 5 points for each void and 3 points for each singleton. (Doubletons are still worth 1 point each.) For example:

♠ 7
♡ K 10 6 3
♢ J 8 4 3
♣ A Q 9 7

If partner opens the bidding with 1 ♡, you'll be delighted to play in hearts because of your fine support. So evaluate your hand as being worth 13 points — 10 HCP and 3 DP for the singleton spade. (It is true that if partner should also turn up with a singleton spade — a bridge disaster known as "duplication of values" — you will have overvalued your hand because you won't be able to ruff any spades at all. Almost always, however, partner will have a few small cards opposite your short suit.)

Now suppose instead that partner opens with 1 ♠. Your support for his suit is terrible, and you don't have a particularly outstanding suit of your own. A no-trump contract is therefore a definite possibility, and you should evaluate your hand as worth 10 points (10 HCP, 0 DP) for purposes of making your first response. If partner later turns up with a second suit that you plan to raise, you can then readjust the value of your hand to 13 points (10 HCP, 3 DP for a singleton with good support for partner's suit).

As you can see from this example, your point count can — and often does — change during the auction. When partner makes a bid that signals good news (such as mentioning a suit for which you have fine support), the value of your hand goes up; while when he does something that warns of stormy weather ahead (such as bidding a suit in which you are very short), the value of your hand goes down. This is a particularly important tip for improving your results at the bridge table.

5. *It's good to have most of your HCP in aces and kings, and it's bad to have most of your HCP in queens and jacks.* Hands with approximately equal numbers of high honors and low honors don't require any special adjustment. However, consider the following hands:

(1) ♠ A 7 3   (2) ♠ Q J 3
    ♡ K 10 7   ♡ A 10 7
    ◇ K 9 7 4   ◇ Q J 7 4
    ♣ K 9 6   ♣ Q J 6

Both hands may seem to be worth 13 HCP, but we have seen that appearances can be very deceptive. Aces and kings are actually worth a fraction *more* than the 4 and 3 points allotted to them, while queens and jacks are worth a bit *less* than their point count indicates. Hand (1) is thus undervalued by four "fractions" — one for each honor — and there aren't any queens or jacks to cancel them out. Therefore it is worth·about 14 points, and you should definitely open the bidding with 1 ◇. Hand (2), however, deserves a reduction because·most of its points are in queens and jacks. It is actually worth only about 11 or 12 points, and you should therefore pass with this hand.

6. *It's good to have a lot of high spot cards such as 10s, 9s, and 8s, and it's bad to have mostly low spot cards such as 5s, 4s, 3s, and 2s.* Although you don't count any HCP for them, spot

cards may well take some tricks — if they are high enough. Therefore, add an extra point or so if you have a lot of 10s, 9s, and 8s, and deduct a point if most or all of your spot cards are pitifully small. You would be surprised at how many contracts have been made because declarer turned up with a 9 or 8, instead of a 4 or 3, at the crucial moment!

7. *It's good to have long suits, and it's bad to have "flat," even distribution.* Long suits often mean extra tricks during the play, and a hand with stodgy 4–3–3–3 distribution isn't going to be much help in that regard. Conversely, suppose that your lifelong dreams come true and you pick up:

♠ A K Q J 10 9 8 7 6 5 4 3 2
♡ ——
♢ ——
♣ ——

Are you going to open with 1 ♠ because your hand counts out to "19 points" (10 HCP, 9 DP)? Certainly not! Intuitively, you will quite properly decide to forget about points in this exceptional case and promptly bid your grand slam. Now extend the same reasoning to the following (more likely) hand:

♠ A Q 8 6 4 3
♡ K 10 9 7 4 2
♢ 3
♣ ——

Don't be misled by the fact that this hand appears to be worth only 14 points (9 HCP, 5 DP). All you need from partner to make game is as little as:

♠ J 10 7 5
♡ Q 3
♢ 10 8 6 4
♣ J 8 3

Therefore, you should not only definitely open your hand with 1 ♠, but should carry a 2 ♠ raise by partner all the way to 4 ♠. The moral: point count seriously undervalues the trick-taking potential of freak hands. When you do happen to pick up a huge one-suited or two-suited hand, you'll be better off counting tricks instead of points. (One word of warning is in order, however. When you have a freak hand, it won't help you much if partner has lots of high cards in your short suits. So don't get too ambitious just because he makes some strong-sounding bids in your singletons or voids; wait until he indicates at least a modicum of support where you need it.)

Some bridge players are "point-count slaves." They count their points once, at the beginning of the auction, and always adhere strictly to what that total tells them. You can see, however, that no amount of mathematics ever removes the need for judgment at the bridge table. And that's an extremely important guideline for improving your bridge technique!

CHOOSING YOUR OPENING BID

When you are deciding whether or not to open the bidding, keep the following scale in mind:

Your Points	Your Decision
14 or more	Open the bidding.
13	Optional. Open with "good" features, pass with "bad" features.
12 or less	Pass.

If your hand merits an opening bid, here's how to choose the right one:

1. *Open with 1 NT or 2 NT if you meet the requirements.* The 1 NT opening bid shows 16 to 18 HCP and balanced suit distribution (4–3–3–3, 4–4–3–2, or 5–3–3–2 where the five-card suit is a *minor*).[1] These hands should be opened with 1 NT:

(1) ♠ K J 6 3
    ♡ A 7 2
    ◇ K 10 8
    ♣ K Q 5

(2) ♠ K 8
    ♡ A J 9
    ◇ Q J 10 3
    ♣ A Q J 2

(3) ♠ K J 3
    ♡ A Q
    ◇ K J 5 4 3
    ♣ K 10 8

The 2 NT opening bid promises 22 to 24 HCP, balanced suit distribution, and high cards in all suits.[2] These hands are good examples of the 2 NT opening bid:

(1) ♠ A K J 7
    ♡ K Q 8
    ◇ A Q 10
    ♣ K J 10

(2) ♠ A Q 8
    ♡ A K 5
    ◇ Q J 10 6 2
    ♣ A Q

[1] *Experts disagree about whether you should open 1 NT with a worthless doubleton, such as 7 4, in one suit. I think you should.*

[2] *Many experts reduce the range for the 2 NT opening bid to 21 to 22 HCP, and open 2 ♣ (forcing) and rebid 2 NT with 23 to 24 HCP. This is in fact preferable for players who are willing to adopt the artificial and forcing 2 ♣ opening bid (see the chapter on "Unusual Opening Bids and Responses").*

2. *Otherwise, with 13 to 22 points, open with one of a suit.* If your longest suit is five or more cards, bid it; in case of ties, choose the *higher*-ranking suit. For example:

(1) ♠ 8 6
   ♡ A K J 7 4
   ◇ 7 3
   ♣ A Q 6 2

(2) ♠ 9 8 7 6 4 3
   ♡ A
   ◇ A 6 3
   ♣ A K J

(3) ♠ A J 7 4 3
   ♡ K 2
   ◇ A K 10 6 3
   ♣ 8

With hand (1), open 1 ♡, and with hand (2), bid 1 ♠. Holding hand (3), open 1 ♠, breaking the tie by selecting the higher-ranking suit.

Don't be reluctant to treat a *very* strong four-card suit like a five-carder, or a *very* weak five-card suit like a four-carder:

(1) ♠ 6 4
   ♡ A K J 9
   ◇ A 10 4 3 2
   ♣ 7 3

(2) ♠ 6 5 4 3 2
   ♡ A K Q J 10
   ◇ A 4
   ♣ 3

With hand (1), the best opening bid is 1 ♡; your four-card heart suit is so strong that you should act as though it were five cards long. The reason for avoiding the 1 ◇ opening bid can be seen by comparing these two auctions:

(A) *You*   *Partner*
   1 ◇   1 ♠
   2 ♡?   3 ◇ (help!)

(B) *You*   *Partner*
   1 ♡   1 ♠
   2 ◇   Pass, or 2 ♡

In auction (A), you must make a very bad bid in order to show your second suit. The 2 ♡ rebid is poor because it forces partner up to the three level if he has terrible hearts and good diamonds, and your hand isn't good enough for such extravagance. (To bid like this, called a "reverse" in bridge terminology, you need at least 17 points.) In auction (B), however, partner can choose between your suits at the two level, and you'll be happy to be that low if he has a weak hand.

With hand (2), you must once again beware of deceptive appearances. A 1 ♠ opening is not wrong in and of itself, for *any* five-card suit is biddable. However, your hearts are so strong, and your spades are so weak, that you should bid as though the hearts were longer. Therefore the correct opening bid is 1 ♡.

Don't, however, carry these exceptions too far. Open 1 ◇ with:

♠ 7 3
♡ J 8 6 3
◇ A K 10 7 4
♣ A J

If partner can't bid hearts by himself, you don't want to play there. And open 1 ♠ with:

$$♠ Q 10 6 4 3$$
$$♡ A K J 4 3$$
$$♦ K 4$$
$$♣ 9$$

Here the difference between your major suits is not great enough to justify breaking the usual rule of bidding the higher-ranking one first. If partner responds 1 NT, you can comfortably rebid 2 ♡, allowing partner to choose the suit he likes best at the two level. Opening 1 ♡ and then bidding spades would get the bidding too high — and would show more hearts than spades.

If your longest suit is only four cards, judgment is particularly likely to be necessary; you should select the opening bid that will make your rebid easiest. The only inviolate rule is *never* to open in any suit of two cards or less, or in a three-card or weak four-card *major* suit. Let's look at some examples:

(1) ♠ Q 5 4	(2) ♠ A 7 3	(3) ♠ J 8 6 3
♡ K J 3	♡ Q 10 4 2	♡ J 8 6 3
♦ A Q 8 6	♦ 4 3 2	♦ A K 10
♣ K 10 8	♣ A K J	♣ A J

With hand (1), open in your longest suit by bidding 1 ♦. If partner responds 1 ♡ or 1 ♠, a rebid of 1 NT will describe your balanced near-minimum hand perfectly; partner will know that you have a no-trump-type hand, but were too weak for an original opening bid of 1 NT. If instead partner responds 2 ♣, raise to 3 ♣. (*Don't* rebid 2 ♦; that would promise at least a five-card suit.)

Holding hand (2), however, you cannot afford to open in your longest suit. One reason is that if partner responds 2 ♦, you'll be stuck; your diamonds aren't strong enough for a raise, a heart rebid would guarantee at least a five-card suit, and a 2 NT rebid would promise a stronger hand with better hearts. In addition, the hearts are pretty weak. Since a three-card *minor* suit may be opened, you should start off with a bid of 1 ♣. This is not a special system of bidding (although some players talk about the "short club" as though it were); it is simply the best choice with a somewhat awkward hand. If partner responds 1 ♦, you'll rebid 1 ♡; if instead he bids 1 ♡, you'll raise to 2 ♡; while if his response is 1 ♠, you will rebid 1 NT. Thus no action by partner can cause you any difficulty.

With hand (3), you should open with 1 ♦. It's best to avoid bidding a very weak four-card *major* suit. Bidding a lackluster *minor* is usually safe, however, for partner will avoid trying for the 11-trick game if any other alternative looks promising. Since you may not open a two-card suit, the diamond bid is the only choice. Only a 2 ♣ response by partner will be awkward, and you can probably survive this unpleasant turn of events by raising to 3 ♣.

(4) ♠ J 8 6 3
    ♡ A Q 8
    ◊ K J 3
    ♣ K J 3

(5) ♠ K Q 9 7
    ♡ K Q 10 3
    ◊ 6
    ♣ A Q 6 2

(6) ♠ 7
    ♡ 6 5 4 3
    ◊ A K J 7
    ♣ A Q 10 3

With hand (4), the spades are once again too weak to bid. Opening with 1 ♣ will solve all problems: You will rebid 1 NT over a red-suit response and raise a 1♠ response to 2 ♠.

Holding hand (5), open with 1 ♣. A good rule to keep in mind when opening 4-4-4-1 hands is to select the suit *below the singleton* — provided, of course, that the suit in question is strong enough to bid. (A 1 NT opening must be rejected because your distribution is too unbalanced.)

With hand (6), the suit below the singleton is hearts. Opening such a weak suit is, however, likely to lead to instant penury. Therefore skip it and choose the next-lower suit; bid 1 ◊.

Selecting the correct opening bid when your longest suit is a four-carder (and when you don't qualify for a 1 NT or 2 NT opening bid) can take some effort and forethought. By planning your second bid before you make your first one, however, you'll make the rest of your auction much easier — and greatly improve your chances of getting to the right contract.

Responding to 1 NT:

AN INTRODUCTION TO THE
LIMITED-BID STRATEGY

A football quarterback who muddles along without a game plan is likely to wind up on the short end of the score (and back in the minor leagues). In bridge, similarly, bidding without any idea of what you are trying to accomplish will cost you a lot of points.

THE LIMITED-BID STRATEGY

Since bidding is the only legal way that you can exchange information with your partner during the auction, you should try and cram as much data as you can into each bid. Your bidding will be easier, and your results will be better, whenever you or your partner can correctly make a *limited* bid — that is, a bid that defines your point count and your distribution very precisely.

To see why, let's suppose that partner opens the bidding with 1 NT. As we saw in the preceding chapter, this highly descriptive bid limits his hand to precisely 16 to 18 HCP and balanced suit distribution. You, as responder, hold any of these hands:

(1) ♠ 7 4	(2) ♠ K 10	(3) ♠ K 8 7
♡ J 10 5 3	♡ 7 4	♡ K 10 5
◇ Q 9 7 5	◇ A 10 8 7	◇ J 2
♣ K 5 3	♣ J 9 5 3 2	♣ A 10 5 4 2

When partner makes a *limited* bid, add the points he has promised to your own. If the total *cannot* reach 26 points, game is *out of reach* and you should stop in the first playable contract you can find. If the total *might* reach 26 points, game is possible and you should *invite* partner to bid it. And if the partnership total *must* reach at least 26 points, game must be reached, and you should either bid it directly or make a forcing bid that partner must not pass.

Let's see how the limited-bid strategy makes responding easy with the example hands shown above. Holding hand (1), you have 6 points and partner has promised 16 to 18 HCP, so your side has between 22 and 24 points. Thus game is out of reach. Your hand is balanced and you know partner's is also, so no-trump should be a playable contract. Therefore, your correct action is to pass.

Hand (2), as we know from the preceding chapter, is worth 8 points for no-trump purposes. Adding in partner's 16 to 18 points shows the total for your side to be from 24 to 26. Game is therefore possible, so you should invite it by raising to 2 NT. This asks partner to go on to 3 NT if he has a maximum (18 points, or 17 points with "good" features), but to pass with a minimum (16 points, or 17 points with "bad" features).

Hand (3) is worth 11 points. (The doubleton jack is a liability; but you have an extra 10, most of your points in aces and kings, and a five-card suit.) Even if partner has his minimum of 16 points, your side must have at least 27 points, which is more than enough to bid game. No-trump will be a fine spot since your hand is relatively balanced, so you should proceed directly to 3 NT. (Note that this bid also informs partner that the 33 points needed to bid *slam* are out of reach, so he has no choice but to pass.)

The limited-bid strategy is useful in many situations, and we'll encounter it again in subsequent chapters. When you use it, keep the following guidelines in mind:

Declaration	Total Partnership Points Needed
Game in a major suit or in no-trump	26 points
Game in a minor suit	29 points
Small slam	33 points

This scale is not guaranteed by Lloyd's of London. A 27-point game may go down because of bad splits or because the hands fit badly, while a 24-point game may come home because of unusually good luck or because the hands happen to fit together particularly well. In most cases, however, the scale will guide you to the proper contract.

SUIT RESPONSES

There is no law of bridge which requires that a bid must show the suit stated in that bid. For example, it is possible to devise a bidding system wherein a diamond bid shows a long spade suit, a heart bid shows shortness rather than length in hearts, and so forth. Such artificial bids (or, in bridge terminology, *conventional* bids) are actually quite popular among experienced players.

There are, however, potentially serious pitfalls when conventional bids are used. If your partner intends that his diamond bid show a long spade suit, but you interpret it as showing long diamonds, you're not going to be terribly happy with your results! (And even great experts have forgotten what conventions they are using — and during important tournaments, at that.) Also, weird conventions designed solely to annoy and confuse the opponents are a clear case of bad bridge manners (and are, in fact, prohibited in tournament play). There is one convention, however, that is so useful that just about all good bridge players use it, and it is called the *Stayman Convention.* Here's how it works:

After a 1 NT opening bid, a 2 ♣ response is *conventional.* It says nothing at all about responder's club holding; he may even be void in clubs. Opener is advised that game is at least possible (that is, responder has at least 8 points), and he is asked to bid a four-card *major* suit if he has one. (With two four-card majors, he bids spades first.[1]) If he doesn't have a four-card major, he bids 2 ◇.

The Stayman Convention has two important advantages. It is the only sensible way to find a 4–4 major-suit fit after a 1 NT opening bid, and experience has shown that such fits usually make for excellent contracts. Also, when you use Stayman, the other responses to 1 NT become extremely simple. A direct response of 2 ◇, 2 ♡, or 2 ♠ shows at least a five-card suit, announces that game is out of reach, and orders partner to pass. A direct jump to 3 ♣, 3 ◇, 3 ♡, or 3 ♠ announces that game must be bid (that is, these bids are *forcing to game),* and asks opener to raise with good three-card or better support but return to 3 NT with only a doubleton in responder's suit.

Let's look at some examples. In each case, partner has opened with 1 NT.

(1) ♠ Q 9 8 6 4 2	(2) ♠ J 10 4 3	(3) ♠ 4 3
♡ 7 3	♡ K 6 4 3 2	♡ 7 2
◇ 6 4 2	◇ 4 3	◇ J 10 4 3
♣ 8 4	♣ 7 2	♣ K 6 4 3 2

With hand (1), respond 2 ♠. Before the invention of the Stayman Convention, hands like this caused terrible problems. The spade suit will surely take several tricks if it is the trump suit but could easily be completely useless in a no-trump contract, so it must be better to play in 2 ♠ than in 1 NT. However, using the methods of the pre-Stayman era, the bid of a new suit was invitational to game — and hence out of the question with a weak hand like this one. The modern procedure is simple and effective: you "sign off" by bidding 2 ♠, which partner passes regardless of his holding.

With hand (2), you should bid 2 ♡. Spades might be a better contract, but you can't afford to investigate by using the Stayman Convention; it announces that game is at least possible and promises a minimum of 8 points. Therefore, sign off in your five-card suit.

Holding hand (3), you must pass. You can't sign off in 2 ♣, be-

---

[1] *This is actually what Stayman himself recommends. A fair number of experts prefer to bid hearts first, however, and some bid the stronger suit first. All of these methods are of about equal merit.*

cause that bid is the Stayman Convention. With an extremely long club suit and a weak hand, you *can* sign off by bidding 2 ♣ and then following with 3 ♣, a sequence that orders partner to pass; but this hand is not unbalanced enough to justify playing a three-level contract.

(4) ♠ K J 8 6	(5) ♠ K J 8 6	(6) ♠ J 6 4 3
♡ 7 3	♡ 7 3	♡ J 7 5 2
◇ A 6 4 2	◇ A 6 4 2	◇ 7
♣ 7 6 3	♣ A 10 3	♣ Q 4 3 2

With hand (4), your 8 points indicate that game is possible if partner has a maximum, and you'll be able to count an extra point for your doubleton heart if you can play in spades. So respond 2 ♣. If partner bids 2 ◇ or 2 ♡, bid 2 NT; just like the direct single raise over 1 NT, this asks partner to continue on to 3 NT with a maximum but to pass with a minimum. If instead partner responds 2 ♠, invite game in spades by raising to 3 ♠.

Holding hand (5), you should again start off with a response of 2 ♣, but you had better be careful at your next turn to bid. Since you have 12 HCP, you know that game must be reached — but partner doesn't! If he responds 2 ◇ or 2 ♡ and you now bid only 2 NT, he will pass with a minimum, and you'll miss an excellent game. If he does bid a red suit, therefore, you must jump to 3 NT; while if instead he bids 2 ♠, you should jump to 4 ♠.

Pass with hand (6). If a little bird informed you that partner held a four-card major, you could reach a superior partial by bidding 2 ♣ and passing his response. Without such friendly (and illegal) assistance, however, you cannot afford to use Stayman, for a 2 ◇ reply will leave you in an impossible position.

(7) ♠ A J 7 6 3	(8) ♠ A J 7 6 3	(9) ♠ A Q 9 7 6
♡ A 10	♡ 7 3 2	♡ K J 6 3
◇ 7 6 4 2	◇ K 6	◇ 4 3
♣ Q 5	♣ 9 4 3	♣ 10 2

With hand (7), jump to 3 ♠. This tells partner that game must be reached and, since you spurned the use of Stayman, that you have at least a *five*-card suit. He will raise to 4 ♠ with three-card support or better and will bid 3 NT otherwise, which you will pass.

Hand (8) is worth a game invitation, but you can't respond 2 ♠ (a signoff) or 3 ♠ (forcing to game). The solution is to bid 2 ♣ first, and then bid 2 ♠ over a red-suit response. With a maximum, partner will then bid 4 ♠ with good spade support and 3 NT with weak spades; while with a minimum, he'll either pass or return to 2 NT (which you must pass).

With hand (9), you can seek out both a 4–4 heart fit or a 5–3 spade fit by using Stayman. First, bid 2 ♣. If partner bids a major suit, raise to game. If instead he bids 2 ◇, however, you must jump to 3 ♠ to warn partner not to pass even with a minimum. (Compare with hand 8.) He will now choose between 3 NT and 4 ♠, depending on how good his spade support is.

Finally, note also that after a 2 NT opening bid, a 3 ♣ response is also the Stayman Convention. The only difference is that since the level of bidding is so high, you should not use this response unless you have enough points to ensure that *game* must be reached.

Responding to One of a Suit

An unlimited expense account is a pure delight, but an unlimited bid by your partner is likely to be more troublesome. For example, suppose partner opens the bidding with 1 ♡. This bid shows anywhere from 13 to 22+ points and from four to seven or eight hearts, and these ranges are so wide that you will usually have to obtain much more information before you can decide on the right contract. Suppose you hold:

♠ K 8 7
♡ K 10 5
◇ J 2
♣ A 10 5 4 2

When you held this hand in the preceding chapter and partner opened with 1 NT, it took you just one bid to reach the best spot. After a 1 ♡ opening bid, however, you'll need to have your wits about you! Consider just three of the hands your partner might hold:

(1) ♠ Q J 10	(2) ♠ A 6	(3) ♠ A
♡ A 9 8 4	♡ A Q J 7 4 3	♡ A 9 7 3
◇ A Q 6 3	◇ 9 7 4	◇ K Q 8 6
♣ 7 6	♣ Q 3	♣ K Q J 9

If partner has a balanced minimum like hand (1), you belong in a no-trump partial. If he has hand (2), a 4 ♡ contract will be ideal. And if he happens to hold hand (3), the winning contract is 6 ♣! To add to the general confusion, he might have a hand that would make a heart partial, club partial, or no-trump game the right contract. With all these possibilities to contend with, it will usually take more than just one bid before you can tell what the final contract should be.

The moral: after partner opens with 1 ♡ (or with one of any other suit), you can't use the limited-bid strategy because you just don't have enough information about his hand. When he makes one of these *unlimited* opening bids, therefore, your best bet is to make the most descriptive bid that you can — the one that will give your partner the most useful information. We'll consider your various choices in order of desirability.

RAISING
PARTNER'S MAJOR

Raising partner's major suit is an excellent choice for two reasons. First, this lets him know right away that a good trump suit has been found, and it ends any confusion that he may have about where to play the hand. Second, major-suit raises are limited bids, so your raise will enable partner to put the helpful limited-bid strategy into operation. Therefore, your first choice as responder should be to raise your partner's major suit. However, raising with terrible support or with the wrong strength is likely to lead to a hideous disaster that will take several rubbers to overcome, so be sure to follow these requirements:

Single major raise: 7 to 10 points, very good three-card or better support.

Double major raise: 13 to 15 points, four-card or better support. (Since partner must have at least 13 points to open the bidding, he will know that game must be reached after your double raise. This raise is therefore forcing to game.)

Triple major raise: Approximately 10 to 12 points, five-card or better support, and freakish distribution such as 5–5 or 6–5.

Let's look at some examples:

(1) Partner opens 1 ♠   (2) Partner opens 1 ♡   (3) Partner opens 1 ♡
  ♠ A 7 6 3   ♠ 7   ♠ 4
  ♡ Q 10 6 2   ♡ K 10 6 3   ♡ K 10 8 6 3
  ◊ 7 6   ◊ J 8 4 3   ◊ A J 9 5 2
  ♣ J 9 7   ♣ A Q 9 7   ♣ 6 5

Hand (1) is worth 8 points, so you should raise to 2 ♠. (If instead partner had opened with 1 ♡, you would bid 2 ♡.) Hand (2), as we have seen, is worth 13 points, and therefore a raise to 3 ♡. Hand (3) illustrates a typical triple raise to 4 ♡. This will almost surely get you to the right contract, and it is likely to prevent the opponents from entering the bidding even when they have a good contract of their own.

The following hand, however, requires special treatment:

        ♠ K J 7 6
        ♡ 7 2
        ◊ A Q 8 6
        ♣ 10 9 3

If partner opens with 1 ♠, you certainly want to play in his suit with such fine support. The problem is that your hand is worth 11 points, and is therefore too strong for a single raise and too weak for a double raise.

The solution is to bid 2 ◊ first, and then support spades as cheaply as possible the next time around. This will inform partner that you have a hand worth a raise to "2½ ♠," or 11 to 12 points and good spade support.[1]

THE 2 NT RESPONSE

If you are unable to raise partner's major suit (possibly because you don't meet the requirements, perhaps because he didn't happen to bid a major suit), the next most descriptive thing you can do is to jump to 2 NT. This limited bid shows 13 to 15 HCP, balanced suit distribution, and high cards in all unbid suits. For example, if partner opens with 1 ♡, respond 2 NT holding:

♠ K Q 8
♡ 7 3
◊ A Q 7 2
♣ Q 10 6 3

With a somewhat stronger hand, you may meet the requirements for the 3 NT response. In standard bidding, this shows 16 to 18 HCP, balanced suit distribution, and high cards in all unbid suits. However, the 3 NT bid uses up so much bidding room that most experts prefer to avoid it whenever possible. After all, slam is very likely when partner opens and you are this powerful; and if he has to make his second bid at the four level, you may well have a difficult time reaching the right contract.

BIDDING A NEW SUIT

If you cannot raise partner's major or respond 2 NT, your next most desirable alternative is to bid a good new suit of your own. The requirements for this unlimited bid are:

New suit at the *one* level: 6 to 17 points, good four-card or longer suit.

---

[1] *To avoid such complications, many players prefer a method called "limit raises." Using this procedure, a single major raise shows 6 to 9 points, and a double major raise shows 10 to 12 points (and is therefore not forcing to game). A conventional response of 3 NT is used to show 13 to 15 points and good support for opener's major. This is an excellent procedure; but since it is not standard, be sure to discuss it with your partner before you try it out at the bridge table. (You are also required to let the opponents know, in advance, about any conventional bids you may be using.)*

New suit at the *two* level without jumping: 11 to 17 points, good four-card or longer suit.

Jump in a new suit: 18 or more points, very good four-card or longer suit.

Some examples:

(1) Partner opens 1 ♡	(2) Partner opens 1 ◇	(3) Partner opens 1 ♣
♠ 10 3 2	♠ A Q 7 4	♠ Q 8 6 3 2
♡ 10 6	♡ 6 2	♡ 6 4
◇ A Q 7 3 2	◇ J 10 6 4	◇ 6 4 2
♣ A Q 9	♣ 7 5 4	♣ 9 7 6

With hand (1), you can't raise hearts or respond 2 NT, so show your good suit by bidding 2 ◇. Be sure to note, however, that bidding a new suit at the *two* level requires at least 11 points.

Holding hand (2), respond 1 ♠. Your diamonds are strong enough for a raise, but minor-suit games require an unpleasantly large number of tricks. Therefore, showing a new suit takes priority over raising partner's *minor;* and since you need only 6 points to bid a new suit at the *one* level, your best choice is to mention your spades.

Be careful with hand (3)! You need at least 6 points to respond and you have only 3 points, so you must pass. The 1 ♣ contract may not be ideal, but it won't be horrible even if partner has only a three-card suit; and responding with such a weak hand is likely to keep the opponents in the chips for weeks to come.

(4) Partner opens 1 ◇	(5) Partner opens 1 ◇	(6) Partner opens 1 ◇
♠ K 10 4 3	♠ A J 7 6 4	♠ A J 7 6 4
♡ K 10 4 3	♡ A Q 6 3 2	♡ A Q 7 6 3 2
◇ 7 6	◇ 7 5	◇ 7
♣ K 6 2	♣ 9	♣ 9

With hand (4), respond 1 ♡. When you have two four-card major suits, bid hearts first. Your suits aren't powerful enough for you to bid both on your own, and starting with the hearts leaves room for partner to mention spades cheaply if he is so inclined.

Holding hand (5), however, respond 1 ♠. With two five-card or two six-card suits, bid the higher-ranking one first (just as you would when opening the bidding). You will trot out the hearts next time if partner doesn't happen to care for spades.

With hand (6), respond 1 ♡. If partner doesn't like hearts, show your spades next time. Bidding your suits in this "backwards" order tells partner that your hearts are longer than your spades. Similarly, bid your longest suit first with either of these hands:

(7) ♠ A J 7 6 4   (8) ♠ A J 7 6
    ♡ A Q 6 3   ♡ A Q 7 6 4
    ◊ 7 5   ◊ 7 5
    ♣ 9 2   ♣ 9 2

If partner opens with 1 ♣ or 1 ◊, respond 1 ♠ with hand (7) and 1 ♡ with hand (8). Then show your other suit the next time. However, this hand must be treated with caution:

(9) ♠ A 7 6 4 3
    ♡ Q J 5 2
    ◊ 7 5
    ♣ 9 2

If partner opens with one of a minor, respond 1 ♠, selecting your longest suit as usual. This time, however, your hand is very weak; so unless partner makes an immensely powerful bid at his next turn, you should forget about showing your second suit.

(10) Partner opens 1 ♣   (11) Partner opens 1 ♠
     ♠ A K J 9 7 6   ♠ 9 3
     ♡ A 7   ♡ 10 9
     ◊ A 6 3   ◊ A K Q J 9 7 4
     ♣ J 8   ♣ K 10

With hand (10), you should jump to 2 ♠; while with hand (11), the correct response is 3 ◊. Hand (11) may seem to be a bit short of the 18 points required for the jump response in a new suit (*jump shift*), but this is certainly no time to be finicky about points! Your hand is worth $7\frac{1}{2}$ tricks and you have an ace and two kings, so you definitely want to be in game opposite an opening bid by partner.

OTHER RESPONSES

If you are unable to make any of the above responses, all is not lost; you have two remaining choices. One possibility is to raise partner's minor:

   Single minor raise: 7 to 10 points, good four-card or better sup-
      port. Usually, relatively unbalanced distribution.
   Double minor raise: 13 to 15 points, good four-card or better
      support.

The other alternative is to respond 1 NT, which shows 6 to 10 points and more or less balanced distribution. This bid will some-times save the day with hands that don't meet the requirements for any of the other choices.

For example, if partner opens with 1 ◇ , raise to 2 ◇ holding:

♠ 6
♡ 5 4 2
◇ Q 10 8 7 6
♣ A 6 4 2

Since you have superb diamond support and an unbalanced hand, diamonds should be much better than no-trump. And raise to 3 ◇ with:

♠ 8 3
♡ Q 8 6
◇ K Q 10 9 5
♣ A K 4

You can't bid 2 NT with a gaping hole in the unbid spade suit, and no other call is attractive. However, respond 1 NT holding:

♠ Q 10 7
♡ Q 7 6
◇ J 10 6 4
♣ K 8 5

Although your diamond support is respectable, no-trump should be a superior contract in view of your balanced distribution. (You should also respond 1 NT over a 1♡ or 1 ♠ opening bid by your partner.)

THE LANGUAGE OF BIDDING:
A CAUTIONARY NOTE

Suppose a man walks up to you on the street and says, "Mrmgrmpf glob furp rumble." Quite naturally, you don't know what in the world he is talking about. As you are about to send for the men in the white coats, he stops you and explains in perfect English that he has cleverly invented his own language and was just asking you how you are feeling today. Even so, the chances are pretty good that you won't want to have anything to do with this oddball.

Now suppose partner opens with 1 ♠ and you hold:

♠ 7
♡ 6 4 3
◇ A Q 9 7 6
♣ 9 8 4 3

Bridge bidding is also a language; and if you decide to invent your own words by responding 2 ◇ with hands like this one, any competent partner will head for the nearest exit. The bid of a new suit at the *two* level guarantees at least 11 points, and you haven't got them. So you must respond with 1 NT.

Therefore, study and learn the requirements for every bid. It will take a bit of effort, but the time will be well spent, for it will keep you from sounding like "Mrmgrmpf glob furp rumble" to your partner.

SUMMARY

When responding to partner's opening bid of one of a suit, your priorities are:

1. Raise partner's major.
2. Respond 2 NT.
3. Show a good new suit of your own.
4. Raise partner's minor, or respond 1 NT.

These guidelines will help you to meet the challenge provided by partner's unlimited opening bid and reach the best contract.

Subsequent Bidding

As the auction continues, each partner tries to simplify matters by making a judicious limited bid. When this happy event occurs, the other player takes charge of the auction by putting the limited-bid strategy into operation, and guides the partnership to the best contract. If, unfortunately, no limited bid has been made, the solution is to follow a list of priorities similar to the one in the preceding chapter.

OPENER'S REBID AFTER A LIMITED RESPONSE

Let's suppose that you have opened the bidding with 1 ♡ and partner has raised to 2 ♡. (The opponents, no doubt grumbling about "never getting any cards," pass throughout.) What call do you make in each of the following cases?

(1) ♠ K 10 3	(2) ♠ 3 2	(3) ♠ A K 3
♡ A Q J 6 5	♡ A Q J 10 3	♡ K Q 10 9 7
◊ 8 4	◊ K J 8 3	◊ A 7 5 3
♣ Q J 6	♣ A 10	♣ 2

Partner's single raise limits his hand to 7 to 10 points and good heart support, so it is time for the limited-bid strategy. With hand (1), you have 14 points, so your side will total only 24 points even if partner has a maximum. Game is therefore out of reach; and since you are in an eminently playable contract, you should pass.

Hand (2) is worth 17 points, so you want to be in game if partner has a maximum single raise (9 or 10 points) but not if he has a minimum (7 or 8 points). You should therefore invite game and leave the final decision to your partner. A reasonable way to do this is to bid 3 ♡, but an even better plan is to bid 3 ◊. Hearts is the agreed trump suit because it has been supported by your partner, so the 3 ◊ bid is *not* an attempt to shift gears suddenly and play in diamonds. Rather, it tells partner that high cards in diamonds will be particularly useful, and that he should add an extra point or so for any diamond honors he may happen to hold. Thus he will go on to 4 ♡ holding:

♠ 6 5 4
♡ K 9 6 2
◊ Q 10 9
♣ K 3 2

Counting an extra point for the highly useful queen of diamonds, this hand is worth 9 points. However, he will return to 3 ♡ (which you will pass) if he happens to have:

♠ Q 10 9
♡ K 6 5 2
♢ 6 5 4
♣ K 3 2

This hand is worth only 8 points and hence falls into the "minimum" category, so he will turn thumbs down on your game invitation. And you'll be in the right contract each time.

With hand (3), you belong in game, even if partner has a minimum, so you should jump directly to 4 ♡.

You should also use the limited-bid strategy after any other limited response by your partner. Included in this category are the jump to 2 NT or 3 NT, the double major raise, the single or double minor raise, and the 1 NT response. Here are some additional helpful hints:

1. After a jump to 2 NT or 3 NT, a double major raise, or a double minor raise, any rebid below game is forcing. Both you and your partner know that your side must have the 26 points needed to bid game, so it would be rather peculiar to stop suddenly in a partial. Therefore, if your judgment tells you that you need to shop around a bit more before deciding where to play the hand, you can do so without fear of being dropped short of game. However, don't push this logic too far:

♠ 7
♡ A K 7 6 3
♢ K J 9 4 2
♣ 10 8

If you open with 1 ♡ and partner raises to 3 ♡, go on to 4 ♡. Slam is out of reach and you have located a fine game contract, so keep the opponents in the dark about your hand. For all you know, the player on your left may be about to lead a diamond and blow a trick or two.

2. If game is in sight after a minor-suit raise, keep a sharp eye out for the possibility of playing in 3 NT. Unless your hand is very unbalanced, you're likely to find the 9-trick no-trump game easier than the 11-trick minor-suit game.

3. If partner responds with 1 NT and game is out of reach, pass

with 4-3-3-3, 4-4-3-2, 4-4-4-1, or 5-3-3-2 distribution. For example:

(1) ♠ A Q 9 6 3   (2) ♠ A Q 9 6 3
    ♡ K 8 4   ♡ K Q 10 7
    ◇ 3 2   ◇ J 3 2
    ♣ K J 10   ♣ 5

If you open with 1 ♠ and partner responds 1 NT, pass with hand (1); your distribution is not unbalanced enough to justify a suit contract. Hand (2), however, has two pretty good suits and two glaring weaknesses for no-trump play, so the best bet is to bid 2 ♡. This asks partner to play in one of your suits at the two level.

OPENER'S
REBID AFTER
AN UNLIMITED
RESPONSE

If you open with one of a suit and partner bids a new suit, you usually won't know enough about his hand to take charge of the auction. Your best strategy is therefore to make the most descriptive bid possible, according to the following list of priorities:

1. Raise partner's major suit with four-card or better support. Make a single raise with 13 to 16 points; make a double raise with 17 to 19 points; and raise from one to four with 20 points or more.[1]

2. Bid a new four-card or longer suit at the *one* level. (Exception: *jump* the bidding if you have 19 points or more.)

3. Bid no-trump with balanced suit distribution. Bid 1 NT with 13 to 15 points; make a single jump with 19 to 21 points. A 2 NT rebid over a *two*-level response shows 16 to 18 points, all unbid suits protected, and a hand not quite balanced enough to open with 1 NT.

4. Bid a new suit at the *two* level. You may only bid a *lower*-ranking suit with 13 to 16 points. With 17 points or more, you may bid a *higher*-ranking suit ("reverse").

[1] *Many partnerships play that a 2 ♡ response to a 1 ♠ opening bid guarantees at least a five-card suit. If you adopt this agreement, three-card support is sufficient for a raise by opener in this sequence.*

5. Raise partner's minor. Make a single raise with 13 to 16 points and very good support; make a double raise with 17 to 19 points and very good support. However, be careful not to by-pass 3 NT unless your hand is very unbalanced.

6. Rebid your own five-card or longer suit. Bid without jumping with 13 to 16 points; make a single jump with 17 to 19 points.

Note that your rebid accomplishes two purposes. It tells partner whether you have a minimum opening bid or substantial extra values, depending on whether or not you jump the bidding; and it helps locate a good place to play the hand as quickly as possible.

Here are some examples. In each case, you have opened with 1 ◇ and partner has responded 1 ♡.

(1) ♠ 7 5
♡ K 8 6 3
◇ A Q 10 6 2
♣ K 3

(2) ♠ 3 2
♡ K Q 9
◇ A K J 6 5
♣ 10 3 2

(3) ♠ 7
♡ K 10 8 6
◇ A K J 7 3
♣ A 6 4

Bid 2 ♡ with hand (1). Raising partner's major takes priority over rebidding your own suit. The single raise shows 13 to 16 points and good support.

Also bid 2 ♡ with hand (2). Your three-card heart support is so strong that you should act as though it were four cards in length.

With hand (3), jump to 3 ♡. Counting 3 DP for the singleton spade, your hand is worth 18 points.

(4) ♠ A Q 10 6
♡ 7 3
◇ K Q 8 6
♣ Q 10 2

(5) ♠ A J 9 7
♡ K 3
◇ A K J 8 6
♣ K 10

(6) ♠ K J 6
♡ 7 3 2
◇ K Q 8 6
♣ A 10 3

Holding hand (4), bid 1 ♠. To be sure, this is an unlimited bid (since it shows anywhere from 13 to 18 points). However, you should always take the opportunity to show a good new suit at the one level. If your side has a good spade fit, this may well be your last chance to find it.

With hand (5), jump to 2 ♠. This *jump shift* by opener shows at least 19 points and orders partner to continue bidding at least until game is reached. A mere 1 ♠ rebid could be passed by partner, a prospect too horrible to contemplate.

Bid 1 NT with hand (6). This shows a balanced hand that was too weak for an original opening bid of 1 NT, and denies a good four-card (or longer) spade suit.

In the following examples, you have opened with 1 ◊ and partner has responded 1 ♠ :

(7) ♠ J 9
   ♡ 6 3
   ◊ A Q 10 8 6
   ♣ A J 10 8

(8) ♠ K 9
   ♡ Q 10 7 6
   ◊ A Q 10 8 6 3
   ♣ 5

(9) ♠ J 9
   ♡ A K 10 3
   ◊ A K J 7 4
   ♣ 10 8

With hand (7), bid 2 ♣. In view of your heart weakness and 5–4–2–2 distribution, no-trump is unlikely to be the right spot unless partner can bid it on his own.

Holding hand (8), however, you should rebid 2 ◊. You need at least 17 points to bid a *higher*-ranking suit at the *two* level ("reverse").

With hand (9), bid 2 ♡. Here you *are* powerful enough to reverse.

RESPONDER'S REBID
AFTER A LIMITED
REBID BY OPENER

If opener makes a limited bid at his second turn, responder then uses the limited-bid strategy to guide the partnership to the right contract. For example, suppose the auction has proceeded as follows:

Opener	Responder
1 ♡	1 ♠
2 ♡	?

As responder, what is your call with each of the following hands?

(1) ♠ A 10 5 3
   ♡ 7 2
   ◊ K Q 6 3
   ♣ 9 8 7

(2) ♠ A Q 8 6 4 2
   ♡ 7
   ◊ J 7 6
   ♣ 5 3 2

(3) ♠ K Q 6 5
   ♡ 10 3
   ◊ A Q 9 6
   ♣ 10 6 5

Opener's rebid shows a 13 to 16 point minimum with at least five hearts, so you should pass with hand (1). Your side can't have the 26 points needed to bid game, and the contract is reasonably playable.

Game is also out of reach with hand (2), but your heart support is so bad (and your spade suit so good) that you should insist on playing in your suit. Bid 2 ♠, which orders partner to pass.

Game is possible if you have hand (3), so invite it by bidding 2 NT. (Don't bid a new suit at the *three* level unless you have enough points to insist on reaching game.) Change the spade queen to the heart queen, giving you three-card support, and you should instead invite game in hearts by raising to 3 ♡.

RESPONDER'S REBID
AFTER AN UNLIMITED
REBID BY OPENER

If your partner opens the bidding and then makes another unlimited bid at his next turn, you are free to pass with a 6- or 7-point mess unless he has made a jump shift. If your hand warrants another bid, keep the following tips in mind:

1. As usual, your first choice is to raise partner's major suit if you can. *Jump*-raise if you are strong enough to be sure that game is reached.

2. *Eight* cards in the combined partnership hands will make for a fine trump suit. If partner has shown a four-card major, raise with four-card or longer support; while if he has shown a five-card major (as, for example, by rebidding it), three-card support is sufficient.

3. A new suit bid by you is forcing. If you have a strong hand but need to look around for a good contract, you can do so by mentioning a new suit; this specifically asks partner not to pass. (Note, however, that a new suit bid by *opener* is *not* forcing, so you can pass his new suit bid unless he has jumped the bidding.)

4. No-trump rebids by you are *not* forcing. A 1 NT rebid shows 8 to 10 points; a 2 NT rebid shows 11 to 12 points; and a 3 NT rebid shows 13 to 15 points.

5. A "preference" bid by you does *not* show any extra strength. Suppose the auction proceeds:

Opener	Responder
1 ♡	1 ♠
2 ◇	?

As responder, you hold:

♠ K 9 7 6 3
♡ J 5 2
◇ 6 3
♣ Q 10 2

You were just about strong enough to respond the first time, but don't leave partner in the lurch! His first suit will usually be longer than his second suit, and you have a definite preference for hearts. Therefore, you should return to 2 ♡. This does not show any more strength than would a pass of 2 ◇.

6. Don't bid a new suit at the *three* level unless you are strong enough to insist on game. An auction like the following one shows a powerful hand and commands partner to continue bidding until game is reached:

Opener	Responder
1 ♡	1 ♠
2 ♡	3 ◊

7. Don't get too high on misfits. Suppose you hold:

♠ J 9 7 6 3
♡ 3
◊ Q 6
♣ A 10 5 3 2

Partner opens 1 ♡, you respond 1 ♠, and partner rebids 2 ◊. You should *pass*. Your spades are far too weak to rebid, your heart support is awful, and any other bid will encourage partner to bid too much. He's on your side, so don't fight him for the contract. If you keep bidding your suits and he keeps bidding his, you'll both have to suffer the sizable penalty that you'll eventually pay out to your delighted opponents.

Most of the time, you and your partner will have a pretty good idea where you're headed by the time responder's second turn to bid rolls around. Remember to use the limited-bid strategy whenever you can, and to follow the suggested priorities when partner has made an unlimited bid.

Unusual Opening Bids and Responses

In this chapter, we will consider those unusual and interesting situations which call for an opening suit bid of more than one.

PREEMPTIVE BIDS

Suppose you deal yourself any of these hands:

(1)	♠ K Q 10 9 8 7 4 3	(2)	♠ 6	(3)	♠ 6 5
	♡ 6		♡ 8 3		♡ A K Q 10 6 5 4 3
	◇ 7 4 2		◇ A K Q J 9 8 7 4		◇ Q 2
	♣ 10		♣ J 3		♣ 8

In each case, your hand is worth a lot of tricks; but an opening bid of one of a suit would be a poor choice. Opening one-bids promise defensive as well as offensive strength, but these hands will be virtually useless unless you play in your long suit. If you open with a one-bid, partner may well double an enemy overcall because he expects you to turn up with a few tricks on defense — and cause a horrible catastrophe. In addition, hands like these afford a golden opportunity to thoroughly (and safely) foul up your opponents' bidding.

Therefore, opening bids of three or four of a suit, and five of a *minor*, are reserved for hands with long and strong suits and little outside strength. A standard rule is to bid *3 tricks more than you are sure of* if you are *not vulnerable*, and to bid *2 tricks more than you expect to take* if you are *vulnerable* (and hence subject to a more serious penalty if the opponents double).[1] Hand (1) is pretty sure to take 7 tricks, so open 4 ♠ if you are not vulnerable and 3 ♠ if you are vulnerable. If your left-hand opponent is looking happily at a good hand and planning to open with one of a suit, your high-level preempt will probably drive him to hara-kiri. With hand (2), open 5 ◇ if you are not vulnerable and 4 ◇ if you are vulnerable. Hand (3), however,

---

[1] *The modern tendency is to be more aggressive, so relax these standards somewhat if you are an experienced player who is good at judging competitive auctions and at bringing home borderline contracts. It's especially desirable to preempt when you are not vulnerable and the opponents are, for any penalty that you incur will cost less, while any game or slam that the enemy might reach will be worth more.*

should be opened with 4 ♡ whether or not you are vulnerable. Bidding 5 ♡ and going down one would blow a sure game, so the opening bid of five of a *major* is *not* used as a preempt.

The following hands require a different strategy:

	(1)		(2)	
	♠	A K J 9 7 4 3	♠	9 7 6 5 4 3 2
	♡	A 6	♡	A 6
	◇	K 10 9	◇	8 6
	♣	2	♣	K J

If you are the dealer (and hence the first to speak), hand (1) has too much outside strength for a preempt. You should therefore open with 1 ♠. A preemptive opening bid could easily cause partner to stop in game when you are cold for slam, or to bid too much in spades instead of doubling the opponents for penalties, because he does not expect you to have so much strength in the side suits.[2]

With hand (2), you should pass. A preemptive opening bid shows a strong suit and poor defense — exactly the opposite of what you have.

When responding to partner's preemptive opening bid, keep in mind that you should usually play in his suit. For example, suppose he opens with a nonvulnerable 3 ♠ bid and you hold:

	(1)		(2)		(3)	
	♠	7	♠	7	♠	Q 10 6 3
	♡	6 5 3	♡	A K 6 5	♡	7
	◇	A Q 9 7 4 3 2	◇	A 6 5 3	◇	Q 10 5 2
	♣	10 7	♣	A J 10 7	♣	K 10 7 3

Pass with hand (1). Partner's suit is at least as good as yours, and fighting with him will only enrich the opponents.

With hand (2), you should bid 4 ♠. After a preempt by partner, count tricks rather than points, just as you would if you were the one holding the freak hand. Partner has promised 6 tricks and you can add 4 more, so game in spades should be there for the taking. A 3 NT response would be a poor choice because you would almost surely get cut off from partner's long suit in a no-trump contract if, as is likely, he has no side-suit high cards to use as entries.

Also bid 4 ♠ with hand (3). You probably won't make it, but why not make life as tough as possible for the opponents? With your

---

[2] *In third position (that is, if partner has dealt and passed and the next player has also passed), an opening 4 ♠ preempt is reasonable. Since partner didn't open, your side is unlikely to have a slam, and your high-level opening bid may cause your left-hand opponent to have a nervous breakdown. However, preempt with strong all-around hands like this one only when you are opening in third position.*

spade support and distribution, you can safely up partner's obstructive action by one level.

(4) ♠ 7 3	(5) ♠ A J 10
♡ K J 6 2	♡ A K Q
◇ K Q 6 3	◇ Q J 10 9
♣ K J 10	♣ Q J 10

Pass with hand (4). You have perhaps 2 or 3 tricks and partner has 6, so game is out of reach; and you have too much defensive strength to worry about blockading the enemy. Usually lower honors aren't all that useful opposite a preemptive opening bid, so don't get ambitious unless you have an ample supply of aces and kings.

With hand (5), you should bid 3 NT. You can tell that partner must have seven spades to the king-queen for his preempt, so 9 tricks in no-trump should be easy. But if he has two small cards in each of the other suits, the opponents can defeat a 4 ♠ contract by taking 2 club tricks and 2 diamond tricks before you can gain the lead. A preemptive opening bid defines partner's hand so accurately that you can bid as though you could see through the backs of his cards!

STRONG TWO-BIDS

On rare occasions, you will hit the jackpot with a hand like:

(1) ♠ A K Q J 7 6 3	(2) ♠ A K Q 7 5
♡ A K 7	♡ A Q J
◇ A Q	◇ K Q J 8
♣ 3	♣ A

To prevent partner from passing short of game (and instantly increasing the murder rate in the United States by one), the standard practice is to open hands like these with a *strong two-bid* of 2 ♠. This shows a hand worth at least 9 tricks, or about 23 points or more, and a strong five-card or longer suit. If partner has a terrible hand (as is likely in view of your powerhouse), he bids 2 NT; with about a sure trick or more and three-card or longer support for your suit, he makes a single raise; or with a new suit containing some useful high cards, he bids his new suit. In any case, you have told him that he must keep going until game is reached.

Here are some useful tips about strong two-bids:

1. It's a good idea to play that if partner responds 2 NT and you rebid three of your own suit, he *can* pass. This allows you to open with a strong two-bid with a hand worth exactly 9 tricks in a suit, and get a plus score if partner has no tricks at all.

With game in your own hand, you simply bid a new suit (or jump to game) at your second turn, since *any* action other than the rebid of three of your suit is forcing to game. And if partner's first response was anything other than 2 NT, even the rebid of three of your own suit is forcing to game.

2. Strong two-bids are almost obsolete among experts, for two reasons. First, they almost never come up, so it is unreasonable to waste four bids (openings of 2 ♣, 2 ◇, 2 ♡, and 2 ♠) on them. Second, the 2 NT response will make the strong hand the dummy if you wind up in no-trump, and the opponents will have a much easier time defending if they can see where your side's high cards are.

Therefore, most good players use a *conventional* 2 ♣ opening bid to show a hand worth a strong two-bid in *any* suit.[3] Responder, of course, must not pass; with a bust, or without any obvious action to take, he bids 2 ◇. Opener now shows his true suit, and the auction proceeds just as though a standard strong two-bid had occurred. This procedure has the additional advantage of enabling the other opening two-bids to be used as preempts (called *weak two-bids*); for example, you can open 2 ♠ (not vulnerable) holding:

♠ K Q J 7 6 3
♡ 7 3
◇ Q 10 3
♣ 8 2

3. The double raise of the strong two-bidder's major suit shows a specific hand: four-card or longer support and *no* aces, kings, voids, or singletons. For example, if partner opens with 2 ♡ (or opens with an artificial 2 ♣ and rebids 2 ♡ over your 2 ◇ response), bid 4 ♡ with:

♠ 7 3
♡ Q J 6 2
◇ 8 6 5 3
♣ 10 7 6

With a strong hand, you would bid only 3 ♡, since the single raise is forcing to game and leaves more room for slam exploration.

---

[3] *Except, of course, for those players who use special bidding systems wherein a 1 ♣ opening bid is artificial and forcing and shows a very powerful hand.*

Slam Bidding

Slam bidding can be difficult. More than a few experts have, to their utmost sorrow, wound up in slam off two cashable aces or lacking the ace and king of trumps; and missing a laydown slam is hardly unusual even in high-level tournament play. So don't be surprised if you have trouble in this area.

One good way to improve your slam results is to make judicious use of four important bidding weapons: the limited-bid strategy, ace-asking conventions, cue-bidding, and the Grand-Slam Force. We'll consider each in turn.

NO-TRUMP RAISES
AND THE
LIMITED-BID STRATEGY

After a 1 NT opening bid by your partner, the familiar limited-bid strategy may indicate a direct route to slam:

(1) ♠ K 10 9	(2) ♠ K 10 9	(3) ♠ K 10 9
♡ A Q 10	♡ A Q 10	♡ A Q 10
◇ K Q 6 3	◇ A Q 6 3	◇ A Q 6 3
♣ Q 10 9	♣ K 10 7	♣ A K 8

You need at least 33 HCP to bid 6 NT, and a minimum of 37 HCP to bid 7 NT. Hand (1) is worth 16 HCP, so you belong in slam if partner is at the high end of his 16 to 18 point range. Therefore, raise to 4 NT, asking him to bid 6 NT with a maximum but to pass with a minimum.

Holding hand (2), your side must have at least 34 HCP, so jump to 6 NT. Since only 6 HCP are missing, the opponents cannot possibly make thorough nuisances of themselves by holding (and cashing) two aces.

You aren't very likely to hear partner open with 1 NT when you have hand (3); but if he does, go all the way to 7 NT. You have 22 HCP and partner has at least 16, so the most your side can be missing is one queen or a couple of jacks.

ACE-ASKING BIDS

To play in six of a *suit*, your side needs at least 33 points *and enough "controls" to prevent the loss of the first two tricks*. Since you count DP when heading for a suit contract, it is quite possible for your side to have 33 points and slam to be unmakable:

You	Partner
♠ A K J 9 6 5	♠ Q 7 4 3 2
♡ K 6	♡ Q 9 6 3
◊ K Q 4	◊ A
♣ K 8	♣ Q J 6

You have 21 points (19 HCP, 2 DP) and partner has 14 points (11 HCP, 3 DP for the singleton with good trump support[1]), so the partnership total is 35 points. However, any slam contract will meet a grisly fate, for the opponents (no doubt chuckling fiendishly) will cash two aces. To prevent such calamities, you must make certain that your side has enough *controls* before you contract for slam. Aces and voids are especially valuable controls, for they ensure that you will gain the lead before the opponents can take any tricks at all in that suit; and kings and singletons may also be useful as controls, for they prevent the enemy from ruining your slam by winning the first two tricks in that suit.

A common procedure to determine the number of aces in the two hands is called the *Blackwood Convention.* After a trump suit has been agreed upon, a bid of 4 NT is *conventional* and asks partner how many aces he holds. He answers as follows:

$$5 ♣ = 0 \text{ or } 4 \text{ aces}$$
$$5 ◊ = 1 \text{ ace}$$
$$5 ♡ = 2 \text{ aces}$$
$$5 ♠ = 3 \text{ aces}$$

Using the 5 ♣ response to show either 0 or 4 aces is not as confusing as it might seem, for it's highly unlikely that your side will get into the slam range with no aces at all. The reason for this procedure is that if the response to the Blackwood 4 NT bid shows that the partnership owns all the aces, the Blackwood bidder can then investigate grand slam possibilities by bidding 5 NT to ask for kings. Responder's answers are similar:

$$6 ♣ = 0 \text{ or } 4 \text{ kings}$$
$$6 ◊ = 1 \text{ king}$$
$$6 ♡ = 2 \text{ kings}$$
$$6 ♠ = 3 \text{ kings}$$

Thus, the auction in our example hand above should proceed as follows:

[1] Note that this is an example of the dreaded "duplication of values." Partner's singleton actually turns out to be worthless, for it is opposite your high diamonds which don't need to be ruffed.

You	*Partner*
1 ♠	3 ♠
4 NT	5 ◇
5 ♠	Pass

If instead partner had shown two aces by bidding 5 ♡, you would jump to 6 ♠; while if he announced proud possession of three aces by bidding 5 ♠, you would be justified in contracting for a grand slam. Note that the Blackwood bidder is in complete charge of the auction, and his final decision *must* be respected by his partner.

Blackwood cannot be used over a 1 NT opening bid because the 4 NT response in this situation is a no-trump raise. Therefore, a 4 ♣ response (the *Gerber Convention*) is used to ask for aces. Opener bids 4 ◇ with 0 or 4 aces, 4 ♡ with 1 ace, 4 ♠ with 2 aces, and 4 NT with 3 aces. If the Gerber bidder discovers that his side has all four aces, he may now bid 5 ♣ to ask for kings (which is answered in the same way); if he does anything else, opener must pass.

For example:

♠ K Q J 9 7 4 3 2
♡ 7
◇ A
♣ K Q 2

If partner opens with 1 NT, bid 4 ♣. If he bids 4 ♡, showing only one ace, sign off by bidding 4 ♠ (which orders him to pass). If he bids 4 ♠, jump to 6 ♠; he may be surprised to become the declarer of a spade contract, but he'll make it easily. And if he bids 4 NT, showing three aces, you can proceed straight to 7 NT.

CUE-BIDDING

Ace-asking bids should be used only when you will know exactly what to do regardless of how many aces partner turns up with. Unfortunately, all too many players use Blackwood and Gerber far too often:

(1) ♠ A K 10 6 5 3	(2) ♠ A K 10 6 5 3
♡ A 8	♡ 10 8 4
◇ 7 4	◇ K Q 10 4
♣ K Q J	♣ ———

In each case, you open with 1 ♠ and partner delights you by raising to 3 ♠. However, your joy will soon turn to misery if you plunge into Blackwood, for you won't have the slightest idea what to do if partner turns up with one ace. Here are two of the possible hands he might have:

(A) ♠ Q J 7 2   (B) ♠ Q J 7 2
     ♡ K Q J   ♡ K Q J
     ◇ A J 8 2   ◇ J 8 5
     ♣ 7 6   ♣ A 6 5

If partner has hand (A), slam is laydown. With hand (1), you have time to pitch your losing diamond on a high heart because your controls will allow you to gain the lead before you have lost two tricks; and with hand (2), the only loser is the ace of hearts. But if partner happens to have hand (B), you had better stay out of slam because the opponents can cash two fast winners.

Therefore, *don't use Blackwood with a worthless doubleton or with a void*, for partner is likely to make a response that will leave you thoroughly confused. Instead, bid a new suit (*cue-bid*) to show partner where your controls are, asking him to do likewise. For example:

(1) You

♠ A K 10 6 5 3
♡ A 8
◇ 7 4
♣ K Q J

Partner

♠ Q J 7 2
♡ K Q J
◇ A J 8 2
♣ 7 6

You	Partner
1 ♠	3 ♠
4 ♡	5 ◇
6 ♠	Pass

(2) You

♠ A K 10 6 5 3
♡ A 8
◇ 7 4
♣ K Q J

Partner

♠ Q J 7 2
♡ K Q J
◇ J 8 5
♣ A 6 5

You	Partner
1 ♠	3 ♠
4 ♡	5 ♣
5 ♠	Pass

Some players would cue-bid 4 ♣ rather than 4 ♡, starting with the cheapest suit in which a control is held. The important point is *not* to use Blackwood; for if partner has precisely one ace, you desperately need to know *which* ace it is. In example (1), his announcement that he can control diamonds is all you need to bid slam. In example (2), however, your return to 5 ♠ after hearts and clubs have been cue-bid clearly indicates severe concern about the diamond suit; and since partner cannot control diamonds either, he stops just in time for you to preserve your plus score.

THE GRAND-SLAM FORCE

The Grand-Slam Force is an extremely useful convention, albeit one little known outside expert circles. It will prevent such calamities as reaching a grand slam without the ace of trumps. It arises in two separate and distinct situations:

1. After the answer to a Blackwood 4 NT bid, a bid of 6 ♣ by the 4 NT bidder is the Grand-Slam Force. (This assumes, of course, that clubs is *not* the agreed trump suit. If it is, the 6 ♣ bid is simply an ordinary sign-off.) It announces that your side holds all the aces and that grand slam is within reach, and asks responder how many of the *top three trumps* (ace, king, or queen) he holds. He answers as follows:

   6 ◇ = none of the top three trump honors
   6 of your agreed trump suit = one of the top three
       trump honors
   7 ♣ = two of the top three trump honors

The 6 ♣ bidder then places the contract, and responder must pass. (If your agreed trump suit happens to be diamonds, responder must bid 6 ◇ with either none or one of the top three honors.)

2. After an auction such as 1 ♠ — 3 ♠, where there is clearly an agreed trump suit, a *jump* to 5 NT is the Grand-Slam Force. Responder bids 6 ♣ with none of the top three trump honors, and the other responses remain the same. Many players extend this idea and use any jump to 5 NT as the Grand-Slam Force, inquiring about whatever suit the other partner just bid.

For example, suppose you hold:

♠ K Q J 10 4 2
♡ A K Q J
◇ A K Q
♣ ——

You naturally open with 2 ♠, and partner raises to 3 ♠. This hand is a bridge player's dream, but it could easily turn into a nightmare at this juncture. Blackwood won't help if partner turns up with one ace, for you won't know which one it is. The solution, provided that you and your partner have agreed to use the Grand-Slam Force, is to jump to 5 NT. If partner responds 6 ♣, you'll have to settle for 6 ♠; but if he bids 6 ♠, you can go on to 7 ♠ with complete confidence that he'll turn up with the ace of trumps.

Competitive Bidding

Your real-life bridge opponents won't be nearly as bashful as the ones in the preceding pages of this book. Instead, they will at times make thorough nuisances of themselves by opening the bidding before you can do so, or by competing over your side's opening bids. In this chapter, therefore, we'll look at some methods for overcoming such interference.

OVERCALLS AND TAKEOUT DOUBLES

If you have a pretty good idea what suit your side should play in even though you haven't yet heard a word from your partner, make an *overcall* of the enemy opening bid. For example, suppose your right-hand opponent opens the bidding with 1 ♡ and you hold any of these hands:

(1) ♠ A Q 9 6 5	(2) ♠ 5 4	(3) ♠ K Q J 9 7 4 3 2
♡ 7 4 3	♡ 7 2	♡ 7 3
◇ K 8	◇ A Q J 9 7 6	◇ 10 8
♣ J 10 8	♣ A 10 7	♣ J

With hand (1), make a 1 ♠ overcall. This shows a respectable *five*-card or longer suit and about 7 to 17 points.

Holding hand (2), bid 2 ◇. You are entering the bidding one level higher than in the preceding example, but your powerful suit and high cards will provide a sufficient safety margin.

As we will see, simple overcalls like these do not absolutely prohibit partner from trotting out a suit of his own; they simply advise against independent action without a sufficient reason. With hand (3), however, you have every right to insist upon playing in your excellent spade suit, and you can do so by overcalling with 4 ♠ if you are not vulnerable and 3 ♠ if you are vulnerable. This is identical to the procedure for preemptive opening bids and shows the same kind of hand — a very long and strong suit and little or no outside defensive strength.

Now let's suppose instead that your opponent's 1 ♡ opening bid catches you with a hand like either of these:

(1) ♠ K Q 6 3	(2) ♠ Q 10 8 7
♡ 7	♡ ——
◇ A Q 4 2	◇ K 9 6 5 4
♣ J 10 8 6	♣ A K J 6

Here you desperately need partner's cooperation in order to choose the right suit to play in. The solution is to make a *takeout double*, which shows 13 points or more and fine support for all unbid suits. This double is not for penalties; rather, it asks partner to bid his best suit.

Be careful, however, with hands like the following:

	(1)	(2)
♠	K 8	7
♡	7 4 3	K Q 6 3
◇	A Q 9 6 5	A Q 4 2
♣	J 10 8	J 10 8 6

If your right-hand opponent opens with 1 ♡, you should *pass* in either case. With hand (1), your suit isn't strong enough for a *two-level* overcall; and with hand (2), you will be in serious trouble if you make a takeout double and partner responds in spades.

RESPONDING
TO AN OVERCALL

Experts disagree as to the best method for responding to overcalls. One good procedure is as follows:

1. The bid of a new suit promises a strong suit but a mediocre hand. Responder is simply escaping a potential disaster with bad support for the overcaller's suit, so the overcaller should not bid again unless he has a powerful hand with support for responder's suit. For example, suppose partner makes a 2 ♣ overcall of an enemy 1 ◇ opening bid and you hold either of these hands:

	(1)	(2)
♠	J 8 7 6 3 2	K Q 10 9 6 5
♡	7 3	7 3 2
◇	Q 4 3	Q 6 4 3
♣	7 2	—

You should pass with hand (1). Partner has promised a strong club suit for his two-level overcall, and his support for your rather shoddy spade suit could easily be worse than your club support. With hand (2), however, you should bid 2 ♠. This warns partner against any further action unless his club suit is truly remarkable, or unless he has a strong overcall and spade support and sees a chance for game in your suit.

2. A single raise of partner's suit is similar to the single raise of his opening bid, showing 7 to 10 points and good support. If he has overcalled with 1 ♡ or 1 ♠, a double raise shows about 11 to 12 points and good support.

3. If you have 13 points or more and are therefore interested in game, cue-bid the enemy suit. This asks partner to make a cheap rebid (as, for example, by rebidding his own suit) if his hand is worth less than an opening bid, but to do something ambitious (such as bidding a new suit) with 13 points or more. Once he has limited his hand in this way, you should be able to use the limited-bid strategy to arrive at a good contract.

4. A 1 NT response shows 8 to 10 HCP and some useful high cards ("stoppers") in the enemy suit; a 2 NT response shows 11 to 13 HCP and stoppers in the opponents' suit.

5. The *jump* in a new suit shows a fine suit and a strong hand and is forcing for one round. The overcaller should raise if he has three-card or longer support; if not, he should either return to his own suit, or bid no-trump if he has stoppers in the enemy suit.

RESPONDING TO A
TAKEOUT DOUBLE

If partner has made a takeout double, use the following guidelines:

1. Don't pass unless you have something like K Q J 10 2 or better in the enemy suit! Partner's double is not for penalties; he is simply showing the other three suits in a single bid and asking you to pick the one you like best. You won't defeat an enemy one-bid unless you can draw their trumps and stop them from scoring tricks by ruffing, and you'll need a long and solid suit to do this. (For this reason, passing a takeout double orders partner to lead a trump at trick one.)

2. Since you must bid even with zero points, you'll have to do something special to alert your partner when you do have a pretty good hand. The recommended procedure is:

> 0 to 8 points: Bid a suit without jumping.
> 9 to 11 points: *Jump* in your suit.
> 12 or more points: *Cue-bid* the enemy suit and then bid your suit.

A non-jump no-trump response shows 7 to 10 HCP and stoppers in the enemy suit, while a jump from the one level to 2 NT shows 11 to 13 HCP and stoppers in the opponents' suit.

3. Show a four-card or longer *major* suit in preference to bidding a minor, even if the minor is somewhat longer and stronger. Game in a major requires one trick less than game

in a minor, an economy that may turn out to be highly desirable in view of the enemy opening bid.

To illustrate, suppose your left-hand opponent opens with 1 ◇, partner doubles, the next player passes, and you hold any of these hands:

(1) ♠ 5 4 3 2	(2) ♠ K Q 6 5	(3) ♠ K Q 8 6
♡ 4 3 2	♡ 7	♡ J 10 3
◇ 4 3 2	◇ 6 5 3	◇ 6 5
♣ 4 3 2	♣ A J 7 6 2	♣ A K 7 2

You should be allowed to demand a refund with hand (1), but don't get so discouraged that you forget to bid 1 ♠! Partner has asked you to bid your best side suit, and you must comply with his request.

With hand (2), jump to 2 ♠. You must take special action to show 9 to 11 points lest partner think you have a mess like hand (1), and a four-card (or longer) *major* suit takes priority over a five-card minor.

Holding hand (3), cue-bid 2 ◇ and then show your spades as cheaply as possible. This will tell partner that your hand is too good even for a jump response — or, in other words, that you have at least 12 points.

NO-TRUMP AND
JUMP-SUIT OVERCALLS

The *1 NT overcall* shows a hand similar to an opening bid of 1 NT (16 to 18 HCP, balanced suit distribution). The only difference is that it absolutely guarantees stoppers in the enemy suit.

In standard bidding, *jump suit overcalls* (such as 2 ♠ over a 1 ♡ opening bid) announce that you are the lucky holder of 18 or more points and a good five-card or longer suit. Such hands, however, rarely come up; so the modern tendency is to use these overcalls as preemptive, showing hands just like the weak two-bid described in the chapter on "Unusual Opening Bids and Responses." When players using "weak jump overcalls" do happen to pick up a powerful hand, they simply make a takeout double first and then bid their long suit to alert partner to the fact that they are worth more than a simple suit overcall.

PENALTY DOUBLES

On occasion, the opponents will crawl (or rush) out on a limb and enable you to precipitate a quick descent by making a killing penalty double. However, spotting good penalty doubles, and avoiding "sucker doubles," may take some practice and experience. Here are some helpful hints:

1. Don't double a small slam with something like Q J 10 9 of trumps and nothing else of value. If the opponents run out to 6 NT and it turns out to be cold, you'll kill yourself (if your partner doesn't get there first). Similarly, it's a poor idea to double a small slam because you have two aces, or the ace and king of trumps. All you stand to gain is 50 to 100 points, and you'll lose a fortune if the opponents escape to a different slam and make it. (Yes, slams have been made off two aces or the ace-king of a suit. Warned by the double, the opponents bid a contract that put the other defender on opening lead; with nothing to go by, he guessed wrong; and declarer quickly rattled off a couple of very long suits and took the first 12 or 13 tricks before the unhappy doubler could gain the lead.)

2. To double an enemy suit contract, shortness in a suit bid by your partner is good while length in his suit is bad. If you are long in his suit, one of the opponents will soon run out and ruff in; but if you're short, partner's high cards will survive the enemy ruffing power — and you may well score a ruff or two yourself.

3. Beware of doubling the opponents into game. A double of a 2 ♣ or 2 ◊ overcall can be somewhat more speculative than a double of 2 ♡ or 2 ♠, for the opponents won't score up a game even if they bring home their contract.

4. Don't double a good opponent unless you have a nasty surprise for him. Holding the ace-king of his suit may seem promising, but he knew perfectly well that he was missing these cards when he bid. Thus he's likely to turn up with a particularly long suit, such as Q J 10 9 6 2. If, however, you hold Q J 10 9 of the enemy suit (and some useful outside high cards), the opponents may well be in serious trouble, because their trump suit is going to divide much more poorly than they have any reason to expect.

5. Don't double with defensive strength against only one contract. If your right-hand opponent overcalls 2 ♡ over partner's 1 ♠ opening bid and you have something like seven hearts to the queen-jack and no other high cards, just pass. A double is likely to chase the opponents out of the one contract you can defeat, and it may also entice partner to make a disastrous double of whatever the opponents bid next

because he expects you to turn up with some defensive strength.

6. Keep the location of your side's high cards in mind. If the player to your *right* has bid a suit in which you hold A Q 10, you're likely to be in fine shape. He rates to hold the king and jack, and you'll be able to swoop in and capture his honors because you play after he does. If, however, the player on your *left* is the one who has bid this suit, things are not so good. He will undoubtedly lead up to his king and jack, forcing you to commit yourself before he does, and you may well wind up with only one trick in the suit instead of three.

7. When in doubt, don't double. It's easier to put up with a 200-point penalty that should have been 500 than it is to explain to an upset partner why you doubled the enemy into game — or, even worse, why your double warned them out of a slam that was going down into one that was ironclad.

No-Trump Play

No-trump contracts usually involve a race to set up long suits. Since there aren't any trumps, you can often turn lowly deuces and treys into powerful winners; for if you lead one and both opponents have run out of the suit, all they can do is discard helplessly. The opponents, however, will try to hoist you with your own petard by turning *their* long-suit small cards into winners, hoping to make you suffer the sad fate of discarding your high cards on their unbeatable low ones. Therefore, your goal when playing in no-trump is to hurry and establish enough winners to make your contract, before the opponents can foil you by setting up their long suits.

HOLDUPS AND THE DANGER HAND

```
                         North
                         ♠ 9 4
                         ♡ A Q J
                         ◇ A K J 9
                         ♣ 10 4 3 2

        West                              East
        ♠ K Q J 3 2                       ♠ 7 6 5
        ♡ 8 5 2                           ♡ K 9 7 3
        ◇ 5 4                             ◇ 6 3 2
        ♣ Q 9 8                           ♣ 7 6 5

                         South
                         ♠ A 10 8
                         ♡ 10 6 4
                         ◇ Q 10 8 7
                         ♣ A K J
```

The bidding:

South	West	North	East
1 ◇	1 ♠	3 ◇	Pass
3 NT	Pass	Pass	Pass

West leads the king of spades. How do you play your 3 NT contract?

1. *Count your tricks.* You are sure of 2 club tricks, 4 diamond tricks, 1 heart trick, and 1 spade trick — a total of 8. You will therefore need to develop an additional trick to make your contract.

2. *Hold up your spade ace for two rounds.* When the opponents are clever enough to attack your weakest suit, refusing to yield your stopper(s) until the last safe moment may pay rich dividends. Observe what happens if you win the first trick and try for the additional winner that you need by playing a small heart to dummy's queen (*finessing* the queen). This would work beautifully if the king of hearts were residing in the West hand, for your queen would hold the trick; but, as the cards actually lie, East would win with his king and return a spade. West would cash his queen and jack of spades, exhausting your side of that suit, and then gleefully lead out his 3 and 2 of spades, winning the race and defeating your contract.

To prevent this catastrophe, you must refuse to win the first trick (the *holdup* play). West continues with the queen of spades, and you hold up again. West pursues his attack by playing the jack of spades, and you now must take your ace.

3. *Avoiding the "Danger Hand."* You now have two ways of trying for the vital ninth trick: you can lead up to dummy's high hearts and finesse the queen, or you can lead from dummy up to your own high clubs and finesse the jack. Which should you choose? (And remember, you can't see the opponents' cards in a real-life situation!)

If you try the club finesse and it loses, West will cash enough spades to defeat your contract. But if you try the heart finesse and it loses, East won't have any spades to return and you'll be safe. And you can figure this out without seeing the enemy cards! West's overcall of 1 ♠ shows a five-card suit (at least) and East followed to the first three spade tricks, so the opponents' spades must be divided 5–3.

Therefore, West is the Danger Hand and must be kept off lead at all costs, since only he can defeat your contract. Losing the lead to East, however, will not be fatal. So, clearly, you should take the heart finesse. As it happens, it loses, but there is no need to worry. Dummy's jack of hearts is now established for your ninth trick; so, when East tries to tempt you into disaster by returning a club, you go right up with the ace and cash all your winners to bring home your game contract.

North
♠ J 2
♡ A 2
◇ K Q J 8 6
♣ 7 6 5 4

West
♠ A 9 6 4
♡ 10 9 8 7
◇ 7 2
♣ Q 10 9

East
♠ Q 10 7 3
♡ 6 5 4 3
◇ A 9 5 3
♣ 8

South
♠ K 8 5
♡ K Q J
◇ 10 4
♣ A K J 3 2

The bidding:

South	West	North	East
1 NT	Pass	3 NT	Pass
Pass	Pass		

West leads the 4 of spades, and you hopefully put up dummy's jack (if it doesn't win a trick now, it never will). East, however, is able to top it with his queen. What now?

1. *Don't hold up.* A holdup in this situation would be suicidal, as East would fire back a spade through your king and the opponents would run the entire suit. Therefore, you must win the first trick with your king of spades.

2. *Attack the right suit first.* It is often correct to attack your longest suit first; and since your side has nine clubs and only seven diamonds, you may think about going after the clubs. However, stop for a moment and count your tricks. You are sure of 1 spade trick, 3 heart tricks, and 2 club tricks; and, once the ace of diamonds is knocked out, you'll be able to win 3 more tricks in that suit. That will bring your total to 9, which is just what you need to make your contract.

The problem with going after clubs first is that if the suit breaks badly and you have to lose a trick, you'll be defeated before you can try out the diamonds. The opponents will happily cash three spade tricks, a club trick, and the ace of diamonds, and winning the rest of the tricks won't be much consolation. You should therefore attack diamonds first.

3. *Play your diamonds in the right order.* If, after winning the the first trick with the king of spades, you lead your 4 of diamonds to dummy's king and East is smart enough to hold up his ace, you'll be in terrible shape. If you now lead a small diamond to your 10 and East plays low again (as he should), you'll be stuck in your hand and unable to play any more diamonds; while if you smother your own 10 by leading dummy's queen, East's 9 of diamonds will turn into a winner.

Therefore, the correct play is to lead the 10 of diamonds at trick two and play small from dummy. If East holds up, play a diamond to dummy's king and continue with high diamonds until he takes his ace. The opponents will now run three spade tricks, but you just discard two low clubs from dummy and a low club from your hand. When you regain the lead, dummy's ace of hearts will provide an *entry* to dummy's high diamonds, and you should have no difficulty taking the rest of the tricks and making your 3 NT contract.

Now let's return to trick one and suppose that West's opening lead is the 10 of hearts. If you're not careful, you'll blow your contract right here! You're likely to need the ace of hearts later on as an entry because dummy has no other sure winners, so take the first trick in your hand and set up the diamonds. If instead you commit the egregious blunder of winning the first trick with dummy's ace of hearts and East is clever enough to hold up his diamond ace for one round, you'll be forever cut off from dummy's good diamonds. The moral: plan out the whole hand before playing from dummy to the first trick — and watch your entries!

GETTING
THE COUNT

West	East
♠ Q J 10	♠ A K 8
♡ A K 2	♡ Q J 6
◇ A K Q 8	◇ J 10 9 7
♣ A J 10	♣ K 9 8

This time you are in the West chair, declaring a contract of 7 NT. Owing to some unfortunate duplication of values, the grand slam isn't cold despite your 38 HCP, and you will have to determine which of your devious opponents has the queen of clubs in order to make your contract. If North has it, you can cash the club ace and lead the jack, intending to let it ride if it isn't covered; but if South has the queen, you must play dummy's king of clubs first and then lead small, intending to put in the jack if South plays low.

To get as much information as possible before making the crucial decision, you should play out your other winners before attacking the clubs. (This might conceivably result in going down two instead of one, but this is a small price to pay with a grand slam at stake!) When you play out your diamonds, South follows suit the first time but discards a small club on the second round of the suit. When you cash three rounds of hearts, South follows the first two times but pitches a small club on the third round. And when you play your three top spades, both opponents follow suit to all three rounds.

Now you must tackle the club suit, with about 2000 points riding on your decision. But wait — what do you know about North's hand? South started with just one diamond and your side had eight of them, so North must have begun with four:

North	South
♠ ? ?	♠ ? ?
♡ ? ?	♡ ? ?
◇ 6 5 3 2	◇ 4
♣ ? ?	♣ ? ?

You also know that South began with exactly two hearts. Since your side had six of them, this leaves five for North:

North	South
♠ ? ?	♠ ? ?
♡ 9 7 5 4 3	♡ 10 8
◇ 6 5 3 2	◇ 4
♣ ? ?	♣ ? ?

And since both opponents followed to three rounds of spades, we can complete the picture still more:

North	South
♠ ? 7 5 2	♠ ? 6 4 3
♡ 9 7 5 4 3	♡ 10 8
◇ 6 5 3 2	◇ 4
♣ ?	♣ ? ?

Twelve of North's cards are accounted for, and your grand slam contract is therefore ensured. Play off dummy's king of clubs, just in case North began with the singleton queen, and then lead a small club toward your hand. If South plays low, you can finesse the jack with absolute confidence that it will succeed. The enemy hands:

(48)

North	South
♠ 7 5 2	♠ 9 6 4 3
♡ 9 7 5 4 3	♡ 10 8
◇ 6 5 3 2	◇ 4
♣ 7	♣ Q 6 5 4 3 2

You won't always be able to get such an accurate count of the opponents' cards. But when you do, it's a great way to impress your partner (and your opponents!) and win a lot of points — and all you have to be able to do is count up to 13.

Suit Play

Ruffing is the key aspect of suit contracts. If you are stuck with some troublesome losers that are about to doom your contract to defeat, you may be able to save the day by executing a well-timed ruff or two. Your opponents, however, will also want to get in on a good thing, and they'll be delighted to ruff away your high cards if they can. So it's important to know when you should hurry to extract the enemy trumps, and when to postpone drawing trumps because other considerations are even more important.

DRAWING TRUMPS
AND RUFFING LOSERS

North
♠ J 10 7 4
♡ A 5 4 2
♢ 7 2
♣ A K Q

West
♠ 6
♡ Q 10 9
♢ Q J
♣ J 9 8 6 4 3 2

East
♠ 9 8 2
♡ 8 7 6
♢ K 10 9 6 5 4
♣ 10

South
♠ A K Q 5 3
♡ K J 3
♢ A 8 3
♣ 7 5

The bidding:

South	West	North	East
1 ♠	Pass	3 ♠	Pass
4 ♢	Pass	4 ♡	Pass
4 ♠	Pass	5 ♣	Pass
6 ♠	Pass	Pass	Pass

When North shows heart and club controls and a 15-point maximum by cue-bidding twice, you properly go on to slam with your fine 18-point hand. After West leads the queen of diamonds, how do you play it?

1. *Count your winners and losers.* As always, see how things

stand before you begin the play. You can count 5 sure spade tricks, 2 heart tricks, 3 club tricks, and 1 diamond trick for a total of 11, so you need 1 more trick to bring home your slam. And you don't have two quick losers to worry about, so there is no need for emergency action.

2. *Start to draw trumps.* If, after winning the first trick with the ace of diamonds, you fool around by leading the ace and king of clubs, East will play a strange-looking card on the second round of the suit. Close inspection will reveal it to be a trump; the trick will be his; and the ensuing diamond return will defeat your slam.

Admittedly, it takes a rather egregious club split for this to happen, but there is no reason to take even a small risk. Start out by laying down the ace of spades at trick two. When both opponents follow, your contract is assured. Finish drawing trumps, *counting* as you go along so that you don't play any unnecessary rounds: your side started with nine trumps, so the opponents began with four. Two of their trumps show up on the ace but only one appears when you play the king, so there is still one left. So you extract the last enemy trump by drawing a third round (either by playing the queen or leading small to dummy's jack, as you wish).

3. *Discard the right small card.* Now you can safely play out all the high clubs, but what do you discard on the third round — a diamond or a heart?

Let's try discarding a small diamond on the queen of clubs and see what happens. The opponents will still get one diamond trick, and you'll be forced to take the heart finesse. Since it loses, you'll go down to a most inglorious defeat.

Now let's try discarding a small heart on the club queen. This will eliminate any possibility of a loser in that suit, since you can simply play the king and ace of hearts and ruff the next round; and all will be well if you . . .

4. *Ruff your loser in dummy.* If you carelessly play some more trumps at this point, you'll ruin all the good work you did previously! Eventually, the opponents will be able to take two diamond tricks because dummy won't have any trumps left to ruff with.

Therefore, play a diamond right now and let them take their trick. Suppose East wins with the king and returns a heart. You win with the king, lead your small diamond and ruff it in dummy, cash the heart ace, and take the rest with good trumps to make your slam contract. The diamond ruff has safely and surely provided your twelfth trick.

Now let's exchange West's 6 of spades for East's 4 of diamonds and try the hand again. When you lead the ace of spades at trick two, West discards a small club. This tells you that East has all four of the missing trumps; and if you draw them at once, you'll also wipe out dummy's supply and never get that crucial diamond ruff. In this situation, therefore, you must postpone drawing the rest of the trumps and play a diamond right away. Suppose East wins with the king and returns a trump. You win with the king, ruff your small diamond in dummy, cash the jack of spades, enter your hand by playing a small heart to the king (spurning the treacherous and unnecessary heart finesse), and play the queen of spades to draw East's last trump. Now you run your clubs, discarding your heart loser, and easily take the rest of the tricks.

The moral of this deal is twofold: ruffing small cards in dummy is often an excellent way to produce extra tricks and avoid losers; and it is a good idea to draw the enemy trumps *if* you won't be cutting your own throat by doing so.

RUFFS AS ENTRIES

North
♠ 2
♡ 6 5 4
♢ 9 5 3
♣ 10 9 8 7 6 5

West
♠ Q 8 7 6 4
♡ ——
♢ 7 6 4 2
♣ A K Q J

East
♠ K J 10 9
♡ A K 3 2
♢ K 10 8
♣ 4 3

South
♠ A 5 3
♡ Q J 10 9 8 7
♢ A Q J
♣ 2

Let's suppose you have been called to the table to replace the original South player who bid his hand aggressively and wound up in 4 ♡ doubled, became deathly ill when he saw the dummy, and had to be carted off to the hospital for repairs. North, who is desperate, offers you a share of the profits if you can make the contract. West leads the king of clubs and follows with the queen. What now?

1. *Don't draw trumps.* If you play a trump and the opponents cash the ace and king and fire back a third trump, you will

have no way to get rid of two spade losers and a diamond loser. Since you will have already lost one club trick and two heart tricks, this will put you down three, and North will be highly upset. Somehow, you must avoid any spade or diamond losers if you are to make your contract.

2. *Ruff your losers in dummy.* Instead, cash the ace of spades and ruff a small spade in dummy. This will immediately get rid of one loser.

3. *Use the ruffs as entries to take the diamond finesse.* In addition, the lead is now in dummy, so you can take the diamond finesse by leading small to your queen. When it wins, ruff your other spade loser in dummy and repeat the diamond finesse. Now, at last, play a trump. East wins and tries desperately to cash a spade; but, thanks to your previous thoughtfulness, you are able to ruff. The opponents will wind up with only one club trick and two heart tricks, and North will be *very* happy.

RUFFING OUT
A SUIT

North
♠ K 10 9
♡ 6 5 2
◊ A K 6 5 3
♣ Q 5

West
♠ A
♡ Q 10 9 7
◊ J 9 2
♣ J 10 9 8 2

East
♠ 7 5
♡ J 4 3
◊ Q 10 8 7
♣ K 6 4 3

South
♠ Q J 8 6 4 3 2
♡ A K 8
◊ 4
♣ A 7

The bidding:

South	West	North	East
1 ♠	Pass	2 ◊	Pass
3 ♠	Pass	4 ♠	Pass
4 NT	Pass	5 ◊	Pass
6 ♠	Pass	Pass	Pass

West leads the jack of clubs and you hopefully put up dummy's queen. East covers with the king, however, and you win with the ace. What next?

1. *Take a quick discard.* Drawing trumps will meet with instant disaster, for the opponents will take their ace and cash a high club to wreck your slam. Anything is better than this catastrophe, so emergency action is called for. Quickly cash the ace and king of diamonds and discard your losing club.

2. *Plan to ruff out the diamonds — and watch your entries!* Things are improving, but you still have to do something about that heart loser. It can't be ruffed in dummy, so your only chance is to discard it on some winner; and the only potential side-suit winner is in diamonds. Here's how the play should go.

At trick three, lead a small diamond from dummy and ruff in your hand. Now lead a small trump. West wins and returns a club, but you are able to ruff. Play a small trump to dummy's 10, lead another diamond, and ruff.

If you have been counting — as you should — you will know that your slam is now cold. The opponents are now out of trumps (they began with three, both of them followed to the first round, and East played a trump on the second round), *and they are also out of diamonds.* (West followed to the first three rounds and East followed all four times you played the suit, so the seven diamonds the opponents began with are all accounted for.) So lead a small trump to dummy's king, play the last diamond, and pitch your heart loser while the opponents discard helplessly.

The technique illustrated in this deal deserves careful study. Ruffing diamonds in your hand didn't produce any tricks in and of itself, for your long spades were always sure winners. But it did enable you to exhaust the opponents of diamonds without losing any tricks in the process and turn dummy's fifth diamond into the vital twelfth trick. *Ruffing out* a suit does take a modicum of counting, and you must also manage your entries carefully. (Note that if you fail to ruff a diamond right after cashing the ace and king, you won't have enough entries to dummy to ruff out the suit and then get back to the good diamond later on. If this isn't clear, play it out a few times and see!) But it is well worth the effort, for it is an impressive way of wresting victory from the greedy jaws of disaster — and one that will clearly mark you as a bridge player with superior technique.

THE MOTHER
OF INVENTION

West	East
♠ 6	♠ A Q 7
♡ A K Q 6 5 4	♡ J 10 9 8
◇ A Q 7	◇ 6
♣ A 6 5	♣ 8 7 4 3 2

While you should never risk your contract for an overtrick (you have too much to lose and too little to gain), it's equally wrong to go down without a fight. Suppose you are playing a 6 ♡ contract from the West chair, and North leads the king of clubs. What is your plan?

Your problem is simple: you have two terrifying club losers staring you in the face, and there is only one conceivable way of avoiding one of them. Therefore, lead a small spade and finesse dummy's queen. It is true that if it loses, you'll go down an extra trick, for you will have lost a spade trick that could have been avoided; but that is a small matter when your contract is at stake. If the finesse wins, you're home; simply discard one of your club losers on the ace of spades. And, of course, avoid the *diamond* finesse like the plague! Play a diamond to your ace, ruff a diamond, lead a heart and overtake in your hand, ruff another diamond, finish drawing trumps, and concede a lone club loser at the end. There's no reason to risk losing a trick to the king of *diamonds*, because you have nothing to gain; even if the finesse wins and you discard one of dummy's low clubs on the ace of diamonds, you'll still be left with two terrifying club losers staring at you in the face.

The moral: like so many other things in bridge, all finesses are *not* equal!

Defense

Defense is generally conceded to be the most difficult aspect of bridge. By improving your technique in this area, therefore, you're likely to gain a real edge at the bridge table.

OPENING LEADS

The opening lead has been called the most important single aspect of bridge by no less an expert than Charles Goren himself. You have less information at your disposal when you make the opening lead than at any other time during the defense, because the dummy has not yet made an appearance. You'll therefore need skill and ingenuity in order to get your side off to the good start that it is likely to need in order to overcome declarer's superior firepower.

1. *Choosing the right card.* The *card* that you select for your opening lead carries a message to your partner about your holding in that suit. Some typical choices are shown below:

Against Suit Contracts		Against No-Trump Contracts	
A **K** 6 4	**10** 9 8 5	A K 6 **4** 2	8 7 6 **5** 3
K Q 7 6 3	K 7 **4**	K Q 7 **6** 3	**8** 7 5
Q J 10 8	Q 8 6 **3**	**K** Q J 9 7	Q 7 **6**
Q J 9 7	**8** 5 (side suit)	**Q** J 10 6	K **J** 10 9 5
Q 10 6 **3**	8 **5** (trumps)	**J** 10 9 5	Q **10** 9 8 3
J 10 9 5	**A** K (alone)	Q 10 6 **3**	Q 8 7 **6** 3

Note that in both cases, you lead high from a sequence of honors but low from sole or unconnected honors. An important difference is that against suit contracts you lead the king from ace-king or king-queen in order to take some tricks quickly before the enemy ruffing power comes into play; but against no-trump you lead your fourth-best card (unless you have a superb solid sequence of honors) in order to build some length winners while keeping the high cards to use as entries later on.

2. *Choosing the right suit.* All other things being equal, it is desirable to lead from a solid sequence such as Q J 10 9 or K Q J. This lead is likely to establish some winners for your side without giving declarer any undeserved tricks. Leading from a broken holding like K J 6, however, may run right into declarer's ace-queen, and present him with two tricks where fate intended him to have only one.

However, one of the fascinating aspects of bridge is that all other things are often *not* equal:

You (North) hold:

	The bidding:			
♠ 6 5 3 2	*South*	*West*	*North*	*East*
♡ K 4 3	Pass	1 ♡	Pass	2 ◇
◇ J 10 9	Pass	2 ♠	Pass	3 ◇
♣ K J 6	Pass	3 ♡	Pass	4 ♡
	Pass	Pass	Pass	

Dummy has promised a long and strong diamond suit that is likely to provide discards for declarer's side-suit losers, so you cannot afford to play safe. The opponents have avoided a club bid like the plague and have refused to play in no-trump even though they own the other three suits, so clubs may well be their weak spot. Therefore, lead the 6 of clubs. The enemy cards:

West	*East*
♠ A Q J 10	♠ K
♡ A Q J 8 7	♡ 10 9 6
◇ 7	◇ A K Q 6 5 3
♣ 10 9 8	♣ 7 5 3

With any other opening lead, declarer will promptly discard numerous club losers from either hand, and losing the heart finesse won't bother him at all. After your killing club lead, however, your side will take the first three tricks in that suit; and declarer will complain bitterly about his bad luck when the heart finesse loses, for his contract will be defeated. Good opening leads often result in unlucky declarers!

When making the opening lead, therefore, *listen to the bidding* as well as studying the cards in your own hand. Try to form a picture of the opponents' hands, and detect where any weak spots may be. You won't always be right; but the more you try, the better you'll do.

SIGNALING

Telling partner in words what you want him to lead is thoroughly illegal. There are ways, however, of letting your cards do the talking.

1. *Attitude signals.* If you want partner to play a particular suit, let him know by playing an *unnecessarily high* spot card such as the 7 or 8 (assuming, of course, that this won't cost you a vital trick later on). You can do this when he leads a high card in the suit, or when you have an opportunity to discard on a different suit. If, however, your attitude toward a particular suit is highly negative because you have a pitiful holding like 7 4 2, play or discard your *lowest* spot — the deuce. This tells partner that, in your opinion, it would be an excellent idea to look elsewhere for enough tricks to defeat the contract.

2. *Distributional signals.* If dummy has a long suit like K Q J 10 3 and no outside entries, the defender who has the ace may desperately need to know *how many* cards his partner has in that suit, so he can then deduce how many declarer began with. This will enable him to withhold his ace until declarer runs out, forever stranding the long suit in the dummy. When declarer's side leads this suit, therefore, playing a high card first and then a smaller one (*high-low*) shows an *even* number of cards in the suit (2, 4, or 6), and playing in the regular order (*low-high*) shows an *odd* number (1, 3, or 5). Distributional signals are so useful that many experts automatically give them just about all the time, refusing to do so only when playing a high card would blow a trick or when declarer is likely to need the information about distribution much more than the defenders.

3. *Suit-preference signals.* Against a suit contract, you may reach a point where partner is known to be out of a suit and you are about to give him a ruff. In such instances, leading the *lowest* card at your disposal asks him to return the *lower*-ranking of the other two side suits, while leading the *highest* card you have requests that he return the *higher*-ranking side suit.

Let's take a look at these signals in action:

```
                      North
                      ♠ 9 4
                      ♡ 8 6 4
                      ◇ K J 10 9 6
                      ♣ Q 10 3
        West                              East (you)
        ♠ 7 5 2                           ♠ 8 6 3
        ♡ A 7                             ♡ K 9 5 3 2
        ◇ 8 5 4 3                         ◇ A 7
        ♣ 7 6 5 4                         ♣ K J 9
                      South
                      ♠ A K Q J 10
                      ♡ Q J 10
                      ◇ Q 2
                      ♣ A 8 2
```

The bidding (West dealer):

South	West	North	East
——	Pass	Pass	1 ♡ [1]
2 ♠	Pass	Pass	Pass

[1] *In* third *or* fourth *position, the requirements for opening the bidding should be relaxed by a point or two.*

West, with commendable loyalty, starts off with the ace of your bid suit. You want him to continue hearts, so you play your 9-spot (*attitude signal*), an unnecessarily high card that tells partner to "keep 'em comin'." He obeys by leading the 7 of hearts to your king, and you return the 2 of hearts (*suit-preference signal*) for him to ruff. You want him to return the lower of the other two suits, clubs, so that you can set up your king before declarer establishes dummy's diamonds for discards by driving out your ace.

Partner dutifully returns a club after ruffing away declarer's queen of hearts, declarer hopefully inserts dummy's 10, you cover with the jack, and South takes his ace. Declarer now draws three rounds of trumps and leads the queen of diamonds, partner playing the 8 (*distributional signal*).

You have won three tricks at this point; and if you grab your ace of diamonds and cash the king of clubs, declarer will easily take the rest of the tricks and make his contract. Declarer cannot possibly have a singleton diamond, because partner is starting a high-low to show an even number in that suit, so you should hold up your ace. Declarer plays another diamond; you win and get out with a heart. Now South is out of diamonds and must play clubs into you, giving you the two tricks that will just defeat the contract.

Good defensive signaling may require practice and experience. It is well worth the effort, however, because it is an effective — and legal! — way to let partner know what defensive strategy will please you the most.

ACTIVE VS.
PASSIVE
DEFENSE

If your hand contains a lot of broken holdings like K 4 3 or A 9 6 5, it will often be a good idea to adopt a *passive* defense by leading a safer suit (such as 9 8 7 5). This is especially true when declarer is struggling grimly to make his contract, and a lead away from your honors and into his may be the only thing that saves him from disaster. However, watch for clues that indicate that you should get *active* and try to take tricks in a hurry:

1. If dummy has a long and highly threating side suit like K Q J 7 6 3, and some outside entries, you had better get busy in a hurry. Given time, declarer will set up dummy's suit and throw away his losers, so go after your tricks fast — even if this involves leading away from one or more honors.
2. If dummy is on your right and has a very weak side suit such as 7 4 2, it is often a good idea to attack this suit even if you must lead away from one or more honors. At worst, declarer will win a finesse that he could just as easily have taken by

himself; and if partner can help out with a high card or two, you may pierce declarer's Achilles' heel and defeat his contract without further ado. In such situations, there is a very useful signaling procedure that you should follow: lead a high spot if you *don't* particularly want partner to return the suit, and lead a low spot if you *do* want him to play it back. For example, when leading through declarer, lead the 8 from 8 7 6 to warn partner not to expect any high cards from you, but lead the two from Q 10 6 2 or K 7 2 to let him know that you can stand the return of the suit even if *he* now must lead away from an honor.

3. With solid suits, an active defense is perfectly safe. Leading the queen from Q J 10 9, or the king from K Q J 10, can hardly give declarer any gifts.

Scoring Table

I. TRICK SCORES (for tricks above book)

1. Basic values:
   Clubs or diamonds = 20 points per trick
   Hearts or spades = 30 points per trick
   No-trump = 40 points for the first trick and 30 points for each subsequent trick
2. Tricks *bid for and made* are scored *below the line*; *overtricks* are scored *above the line.*
3. Game= 100 points *below the line.* It may be made in a single deal; or, provided that the opponents do not themselves make game in the meantime, by building up two or more *part-scores.*
4. The first side to win *two games* wins the *rubber.*
5. If a doubled contract is made, multiply only the below-the-line trick score by 2; if a redoubled contract is made, multiply only the below-the-line trick score by 4. If overtricks are made, see "Bonuses," below.

II. BONUSES

1. Winning the rubber:
   500 points if the opponents are vulnerable
   700 points if the opponents are not vulnerable
2. Small slam:
   500 points if you are not vulnerable
   750 points if you are vulnerable
3. Grand slam:
   1000 points if you are not vulnerable
   1500 points if you are vulnerable
4. Honors in one hand:
   100 points for four trump honors
   150 points for five trump honors
   150 points for four aces at no-trump
5. For making a doubled or redoubled contract: 50 points
6. Doubled overtricks:
   100 points per trick if you are not vulnerable
   200 points per trick if you are vulnerable
   For *redoubled* overtricks, multiply these values by 2.
7. When a rubber is unfinished:
   300 points for a game
   50 points for a part-score

III. PENALTIES:

	Not Vulnerable		Vulnerable	
	First Trick	Each Subsequent Trick	First Trick	Each subsequent Trick
Undoubled	50	50	100	100
Doubled	100	200	200	300
Redoubled	200	400	400	600

Recommended Reading

Books marked with an asterisk (*) are for advanced players only.

Darvas, Robert, & Hart, Norman deV. *Right Through The Pack* London: George Allen & Unwin, 1957.

Ewen, Robert B. *Opening Leads* Englewood Cliffs, N.J.: Prentice-Hall, 1970.

Ewen, Robert B. *Doubles for Takeout, Penalties, and Profit in Contract Bridge* Englewood Cliffs, N.J.: Prentice-Hall, 1973.

Frey, Richard L., Truscott, Alan F., & Smith, Thomas M. (eds.) *The Official Encyclopedia of Bridge* (Revised Ed.) New York: Crown, 1971.

Goren, Charles H. *Goren's Bridge Complete* (Revised Ed.) New York: Doubleday, 1973.

Kantar, Edwin B. *Introduction to Declarer's Play* Englewood Cliffs, N.J.: Prentice-Hall, 1968.

Kantar, Edwin B. *Introduction to Defender's Play* Englewood Cliffs, N.J.: Prentice-Hall, 1968.

*Kelsey, H. W. *Killing Defense at Bridge* New York: Hart, 1970.

Lawrence, Mike. *How to Read Your Opponent's Cards* Englewood Cliffs, N.J.: Prentice-Hall, 1973.

*Miles, Marshall. *How to Win at Duplicate Bridge* Jericho, N.Y.: Exposition Press, 1957.

Miles, Marshall. *All Fifty-Two Cards* Jericho, N.Y.: Exposition Press, 1963.

Mollo, Victor. *Bridge in the Menagerie* New York: Hawthorn, 1967.

Mollo, Victor, & Gardener, Nico. *Card Play Technique: The Art of Being Lucky* London: George Newnes, 1955.

*Reese, Terence. *Master Play* New York: Cornerstone, 1972.

Reese, Terence. *Play Bridge with Reese* New York: Barnes & Noble, 1962.

Reese, Terence. *Develop Your Bidding Judgment* New York: Cornerstone, 1964.

*Rubens, Jeff. *The Secrets of Winning Bridge* New York: Grosset & Dunlap, 1969.

Sheinwold, Alfred. *Five Weeks to Winning Bridge* New York: Permabooks, 1960.

Simon, S. J. *Why You Lose at Bridge* New York: Cornerstone, 1961.

Index

About the Author

Robert B. Ewen is a Life Master of the American Contract Bridge League. He is the author of the best-selling bridge classic *Opening Leads* and the recently released *Doubles for Takeout, Penalties, and Profit in Contract Bridge*, both published by Prentice-Hall. He is also a member of the Charles Goren Editorial Board, under whose auspices he produced the highly successful *Charles Goren Presents the Precision System*, and is a frequent contributor to the *ACBL Bulletin, The Bridge World,* and *Popular Bridge*. Mr. Ewen was formerly an associate professor of psychology and assistant department chairman at New York University, where he earned a reputation as an excellent teacher. He is presently residing in Miami, Florida.